CONTENTS

ACKNOWLEDGEMENTS

I decided to write this book on the Cold War after reading *From Yalta to Vietnam* by David Horowitz. His book, published by MacGibbon and Kee, first exposed for me the inadequacies of the current orthodoxy. It also introduced me to D. F. Fleming's *The Cold War and its Origins* (Allen and Unwin). Fleming's book is so comprehensive that at one point I felt it would be otiose to continue my own work. I suffered similar qualms when Stephen Ambrose published his *Rise to Globalism: American Foreign Policy Since 1938* (Pelican History of the US Vol. 8). However, Ambrose not only answered many questions but also opened up some new lines of investigation.

While my principal debt is to Horowitz, Fleming and Ambrose, I am also greatly indebted to the following: Gar Alperovitz, *Atomic Diplomacy: Hiroshima and Potsdam* (Secker and Warburg); E. H. Carr, *The Bolshevik Revolution 1917–1923* Vol. 3 (Macmillan); I. Deutscher, *Stalin* (Oxford University Press); R. W. Pethybridge, *A History of Postwar Russia* (Allen and Unwin); F. B. Singleton, *Background to Eastern Europe* (Pergamon Press Ltd.); H. K. Smith, *The State of Europe* (Cresset Press).

In addition I wish to thank the other authors whose books and articles are listed in the bibliography and to acknowledge the help of the anonymous benefactors who compile Keesing's Contemporary Archives.

The photographs have been reproduced by permission of the following: the Proprietors of *Punch*, Camera Press, Cartoon by David Low by arrangement with the Trustees and the *London Evening Standard*, Novosti Press Agency, Paul Popper, Imperial War Museum, Keystone Press Agency, National Film Archive, Phoebus Publishing Company, Radio Times Hulton Picture Library, United Press International, Fox Photos.

Finally I thank the library staff of Kingsway College for Further Education who made it possible for me to consult many of the books I have mentioned.

Hugh Higgins
April 1973

Studies in Modern History

THE COLD WAR

THE
COLD WAR
HUGH HIGGINS

HEINEMANN EDUCATIONAL BOOKS

Heinemann Educational Books Ltd
22 Bedford Square, London WC1B 3HH
LONDON EDINBURGH MELBOURNE AUCKLAND
HONG KONG SINGAPORE KUALA LUMPUR NEW DELHI
IBADAN NAIROBI JOHANNESBURG
EXETER (NH) KINGSTON PORT OF SPAIN

ISBN 0 435 31397 5

Set, printed and bound in Great Britain by
Fakenham Press Limited, Fakenham, Norfolk

INTRODUCTION

Gordon Leff has pointed out that: 'Periodization is indispensable to historical understanding of any kind.' Defining a period is, however, no easy task. There are various opinions about the chronology of the Cold War. Some historians claim that it began in 1917, others that it started only in 1947. Its terminal date is also a matter of dispute: in the view of some observers it is still being waged. The period considered in this book begins in 1917 and ends in 1960.

The Bolshevik Revolution of November 1917, which marked the emergence of Communism as a state power, seems a logical starting point: in the years following it we can see the origins of the Cold War. The most intense period of ideological conflict – the Cold War proper – was during the decade after 1945; this account concentrates on those years. In that period China became the second major enemy of the Western powers. It formed part of the monolithic Communist bloc which Truman and his successors sought to contain. The Cold War conflict remained two-sided: on the one hand the Western and on the other the Communist world. During the years after 1956, however, a rift appeared in the monolith. The Sino–Soviet split created, in Crankshaw's phrase, a new Cold War.* The conflict was no longer two-sided but triangular. To the antagonism between the West and the Communists was added the dispute between Moscow and Peking. By 1960 the divisions within the Communist world had broken the pattern of the classic Cold War confrontation between Communism and its enemies. It took some time for the significance of the split to be appreciated. In 1962 the Cuban missile crisis seemed to emphasize the continuing hostility between the Soviet Union and the USA. It was certainly one of the most dangerous clashes in the post-1945 period. Its effect was, however, to emphasize how completely Khrushchev was committed to a policy of peaceful co-existence. He chose humiliation rather than ultimate confrontation. Paradoxically, the

* See E. Crankshaw, *The New Cold War: Moscow v. Pekin.* (Penguin, 1963.)

crisis in some ways brought the USA and the Soviet Union closer together (literally with the 'hot line' between Moscow and Washington). On the other hand it pushed Russia and China farther apart. Viewed in the context of the 1960s as a whole it was an aberration from the policy of co-existence rather than a continuation of the old Cold War.

In the following year, 1963, the Soviet Union, the USA, and Britain initialled a partial nuclear test-ban treaty. A Chinese statement claimed that the treaty reflected 'the ugly face of US imperialism . . . as well as the servile features of those who are warmly embracing American imperialism'.* In 1965 the Chinese dissented from Soviet policy on the central issue of Vietnam, alleging that the Russians were prepared to do 'a political deal with US imperialism'.† Despite the ever-increasing American commitment in the Vietnam War, which might have been expected to unify the Communist bloc, Sino–Soviet relations became more and more strained. In March 1969 armed clashes between Soviet and Chinese frontier guards caused considerable loss of life. (Despite half a century of mutual antagonism the Americans and the Russians have never fired on each other.) Those events seem to indicate that the Sino–Soviet split caused a fundamental change in international relations that made the old Cold War concepts outmoded. Accordingly, this account ends in 1960, when the split became irreparable.

In addition to the difficulty of determining its duration, the student of the Cold War is confronted by other problems. One of them is the unavailability, for the general reader, of Soviet and Chinese sources. Communist historians have published much more than is generally recognized but much of their material is accessible only to the specialists. Thanks to the closed nature of the societies in Russia and China a great deal remains hidden even from them. Until much more is revealed by Moscow and Peking we must appreciate that some questions, such as the motives behind the Korean War, cannot be answered definitively.

Perhaps the greatest problem for the student is the variety of interpretations of the Cold War by Western historians. We may rejoice that our society is so much more open than the Soviet system that publication here does not depend on the whim of face-

---

* Keesings, *The Sino–Soviet Dispute*, p. 60.
† Ibid, p. 79. (Contemporary Archives, 1970.)

less censors. If we assume, however, that freedom from constraint guarantees objectivity we are deluding ourselves. A commonly held view is that Western historians are objective and that only in Communist countries is history falsified for political purposes. It is true that here it is rare to find the deliberate re-writing of history that is common in the Soviet Union. There is no recent parallel in Britain to the notorious *History of the Communist Party of the Soviet Union*, commissioned, and in part written, by Stalin, which was published in 1938. Its treatment of the career of Trotsky is only one example of the distortion, omission and utter fabrication that characterized the whole book. Such subservience by the historian to the party line is not found here. Nevertheless Western historians do distort and do omit facts that do not accord with their own interpretation.

In the words of Horowitz: '. . . the claim to be scientifically objective or detached is only a smoke-screen which, paradoxically, is more likely to blind the historian himself than anyone else'.★ There is indeed no such thing as completely objective history. Historians, like everyone else, are affected by their upbringing and their environment. We must understand that, for example, the 'truth' about the Bolshevik Revolution for a right-wing historian differs from the 'truth' as seen from the left. Churchill's view is a world away from that of Isaac Deutscher, although both were honest, even brilliant, historians. Students of the Cold War are constantly faced by such discrepancies. Trying to arrive at what we hope is a 'true' version demands a constant awareness of the bias that is present in ourselves and in those whose books we read. Bias can scarcely be eradicated but it can be recognized and taken into account. One of the aims of this book is to show how the events of the Cold War have been variously interpreted. This is not to say that there will be no distortions even in an attempt to examine other distortions. At least the reader should be constantly reminded of the fact that one man's truth may be another's falsehood.

★ Horowitz, *From Yalta to Vietnam*, Preface to 1971 Edition, p. 18. (Penguin, 1971.)

One

THE SOVIETS AND THE WEST

The Cold War originated with the Bolshevik Revolution. In November 1917 the Bolsheviks seized control of Petrograd, the capital of Russia, and their régime was quickly accepted in many other parts of the country. Shortly after he gained control Lenin, the Bolshevik leader, stated: 'We shall now proceed to construct the socialist order.'[1] That promise to his supporters was a challenge to his enemies. It helps to explain why there was hostility between Russia and the rest of the world. Russia became the first socialist state and was seen as a threat to all other states which were not socialist.

There is often some confusion over the words socialist and Communist. In the West we usually describe Russia as a Communist country. Thus we recognize that its system of government is based on the ideas of Karl Marx.[2] In 1848 Marx and his friend Engels published the *Communist Manifesto* in which they predicted the collapse of capitalism and the triumph of Communism. Although the Russians call themselves Communists they say that their country is socialist; they have not yet attained the kind of society envisaged by Marx. Slogans on the buildings in Moscow proclaim that they are moving towards the victory of Communism. There is not space here to examine fully the system of ideas, the ideology, on which the Russians have planned their development.[3] We can, however, recognize that from the beginning their ideas were repugnant to many people in the West. One of their severest critics was Winston Churchill.

A recent biographer has indicated how bitterly hostile he was to the new socialist state. 'He loathed "the foul baboonery" of Bolshevism, described Lenin as "the monster crawling down from his pyramid of skulls", and was eager to assist as Minister of Munitions in the rapid supply of surplus military equipment to the anti-Bolshevik forces.'[4] His attitude did not soften when the aid he supplied failed to dislodge the Bolsheviks. ' "The theories of Lenin

1

and Trotsky", he declared in January 1920, ". . . have driven man from the civilization of the twentieth century into a condition of barbarism worse than the Stone Age, and left him the most awful and pitiable spectacle in human experience, devoured by vermin, racked by pestilence, and deprived of hope." [5] More than most, Churchill realized the danger that faced the rest of the world. In 1924 he warned: 'From the earliest moment of its birth the Russian Bolshevist Government has declared its intention of using all the power of the Russian Empire to promote a world revolution. Their agents have penetrated into every country. Everywhere they have endeavoured to bring into being the "germ cells" from which the cancer of Communism should grow . . .' [6]

The Western way of life was equally repugnant to the Bolsheviks. Bukharin, one of the ablest young members of the Party, presents a picture which may appear grossly distorted to Westerners but seemed obvious to the revolutionaries in Russia: 'The children's heads are stuffed with fables about the revolution and the revolutionary movement. Emperors, kings and industrial magnates are glorified. In the churches, the priests, who are salaried by the State, preach that all authority comes from God. Day after day, the bourgeois newspapers trumpet these lies, whilst working-class papers are in most cases suppressed by the capitalist State . . . A German imperialist bandit wrote: "We do not only need the soldiers' legs, but also their brains and their hearts." The bourgeois State, in like manner, aims at educating the workers so that they may resemble domestic animals who will work like horses, and eat humble pie.' [7] Such was the system that had provoked the revolution. The future was to be very different: 'What Marx prophesied is being fulfilled under our very eyes. The old order is collapsing. The crowns are falling from the heads of kings and emperors. Everywhere the workers are advancing towards revolution, and towards the establishment of soviet rule.' [8]

That confident assertion was echoed fearfully in the West. Lloyd George, the British Prime Minister, issued a warning in 1919 to the Western leaders: 'The whole of Europe is filled with the spirit of revolution. There is a deep sense not only of discontent but of anger and revolt amongst the workmen against pre-war conditions. The whole existing order in its political, social and economic aspects is questioned by the masses of the population from one end of Europe to the other.' [9]

There had been no such fears in the days immediately after the Bolshevik Revolution: Western observers felt that Lenin and Trotsky would not last long. Even experienced diplomats like Lord Robert Cecil thought they were merely German agents and the British *Morning Post* expected news of their rejection by patriotic Russians at any moment. Only gradually was it appreciated that the Bolsheviks were going to retain their power. That appreciation was followed by the fear that Lenin might do a deal with the Germans. The Bolsheviks had seized power promising land, peace and bread to the Russian people. They had denounced the war as an imperialist war and in December 1917 had agreed armistice terms with the Germans, who were poised to attack Russia.

For a time Lloyd George considered that it might be possible, despite that armistice, to form an alliance with the Bolsheviks against the Germans. While the Bolshevik leaders distrusted Anglo–American capitalism they were, at the beginning of 1918, even more fearful of German militarism. Given the complete collapse of the Russian army, the German High command might easily destroy the Bolshevik government. Thus, R. H. Bruce Lockhart, a British diplomat with experience of Russia, was sent as the head of a special mission to establish unofficial relations with the Bolsheviks.[10]

In an interview with Lockhart at the end of February 1918, Lenin explained the Bolshevik position: 'So long . . . as the German danger exists, I am prepared to risk a co-operation with the Allies, which should be temporarily advantageous to both of us. In the event of German aggression, I am even willing to accept military support. At the same time I am quite convinced that your Government will never see things in this light. It is a reactionary Government. It will co-operate with the Russian reactionaries.'[11] To what extent co-operation between the Bolsheviks and the Western powers was feasible is a matter of dispute.[12] In fact it did not take place. The Bolsheviks on 3 March 1918 signed the Treaty of Brest-Litovsk. By it they surrendered large areas of the former Russian Empire including Finland, Estonia, Latvia, Lithuania, part of territory once controlled by Poland and the Ukraine. Neither the Bolsheviks nor the Germans accepted the treaty as a permanent settlement. It was to be broken as often as possible by both signatories for their individual advantage.[13] To the Western powers it was a signal to destroy the Bolsheviks and put in their place a government that would continue the war against Germany.

The result was allied intervention against Russia.[14] From 1918 to 1920 a desperate war was fought. On one side were the Bolsheviks. Against them were supporters of the tsarist régime, Russian liberals, various socialist and anarchist groups who considered the Bolsheviks too dictatorial and an array of foreigners. British, American, French, Japanese, Italian and Czech troops fought by the side of the 'white' Russians to smash the Bolsheviks. Eight months after the intervention began the Germans, fighting against the Allies on the Western Front, were forced to sue for an armistice which was in effect an admission of defeat. Although the principal justification for waging war against Russia, that Brest-Litovsk had given the Germans a free hand in the West, had thus ceased to exist, the intervention continued.

To the Soviets the reason for its continuation was clear. A Soviet pamphlet addressed to British and American troops stated: 'If there was ever the slightest doubt as to the intentions of the Allied Governments, there can be none now. The purpose of the Allied invasion of Russia is to crush the Socialist Republic and to re-establish the reign of capitalism and landlordism.'[15] Western historians have suggested that, in fact, the ideological motives behind the intervention have been exaggerated. They point out that Lloyd George was only a half-hearted interventionist, perhaps more concerned with resisting Churchill in the British Cabinet than in fighting the Bolsheviks in the Russian battlefield. On 22 September 1919 he accused Churchill, the principal British supporter of intervention, of being 'obsessed by Russia' and continued '. . . you won't find another responsible person in the whole land who will take your view, why waste your energy and your usefulness on this vain fretting which completely paralyses you for other work?'[16]

Kennan has indicated that Woodrow Wilson, the American President, agreed with the view of his Secretary of State that, with the signing of the armistice, US forces should pull out of Russia: 'If he had felt that the decision was his to make, he would have withdrawn the force immediately. But throughout the winter and spring of 1919 he was at the Paris Peace Conference, and he did not wish to take action independently until some general policy toward Russia had been thrashed out with the other Allies.'[17]

However, while the Allied leaders did not persist in intervention, it cannot be doubted that one of their original motives had been to destroy the Bolsheviks, in addition to neutralizing German influence in Russia. Ullman, one of the main authorities on the intervention, says: 'By the following month, [August 1918] when a British, French, and American force under British command landed at Archangel and Japanese and American troops began to flow into Siberia . . . it was openly acknowledged that they were going into combat against the Bolsheviks, not the Germans, who had already begun withdrawing troops from Finland and the Ukraine in order to bolster their crumbling positions in the West.'[18] Analysing Wilson's sending of troops to Siberia, Levin comments on 'the desire of the President and his advisers to support these Russian elements, favourable to a pro-Allied order of liberal nationalism, whom Wilsonians felt were menaced, in differing and yet . . . interrelated ways, by both German imperialism and Bolshevism.'[19]

Furthermore the later decision to recall the troops could not undo the effects of intervention in the situation in Russia. The evidence of two Western officials on this point is significant.

Bruce Lockhart, who had first hand experience of the impact of intervention, commented: 'For the intensification of that bloody struggle [the Russian Civil War] Allied intervention, with the false hopes it raised, was largely responsible. I do not say that a policy of abstention from interference in the internal affairs of Russia would have altered the course of the Bolshevik revolution. I do suggest that our intervention intensified the terror and increased the bloodshed.'[20] An American observer has indicated that in the course of that struggle the Bolshevik régime was almost liquidated: 'Bullitt . . . thus described the prevailing mood at the Paris Conference in April 1919: "Kolchak [one of the White leaders] made a 100-mile advance, and immediately the entire press of Paris was . . . announcing that Kolchak would be in Moscow within two weeks; and therefore everyone in Paris, including I regret to say members of the American commission, began to grow very lukewarm about peace in Russia, because they thought Kolchak would arrive in Moscow and wipe out the Soviet Government." '[21]

Although Allied troops played a comparatively insignificant part in the war against the Bolsheviks, Allied financial and material aid created forces which nearly destroyed the revolution. Without such help Kolchak would never have been within striking distance of

PUNCH, OR THE LONDON CHARIVARI.—June 4, 1919.

THE BEAR TURNS.

'Punch's' view of the Civil War in June 1919 – the Russian bear turns against the Bolsheviks.

Moscow. We do not know precisely the extent of that aid but it was certainly considerable. 'According to a memorandum issued by Winston Churchill on September 15, 1919, Great Britain to that date had spent nearly £100,000,000 sterling and France between £30,000,000 and £40,000,000 on General Denikin alone. The British campaign in the north cost £18,000,000. The Japanese admitted the expenditure of 900,000,000 yen on the maintenance of their 70,000 troops in Siberia.'[22] Of course the Bolsheviks did not know the details of the assistance but they could see its results. The Siberians had a popular song that made the point:

> Uniform British,
> Epaulettes from France,
> Japanese tobacco,
> Kolchak leads the dance.
> Uniform in tatters,
> Epaulettes all gone,
> So is the tobacco,
> Kolchak's day is done.[23]

By the time Kolchak and the other anti-Bolshevik forces had been defeated Russia was in a state of chaos. Millions had died in battle or through disease and starvation.

The intervention was the first confrontation between Communism as a state power and its opponents. It cast a long shadow. Western statesmen regretted their failure to destroy unscrupulous enemies who openly proclaimed their policy of overthrowing established governments throughout the world. In March 1919 Lenin said: 'We are living not merely in a state, but in a *system of states*; and it is inconceivable that the Soviet republic should continue to exist for a long period side by side with imperialist states. Ultimately one or the other must conquer. Until this end occurs a number of terrible clashes between the Soviet republic and bourgeois states is inevitable.'[24] During the same month a Communist International was established in Moscow. It appealed to the workers of all countries to support the Soviet régime by all available means, including, if necessary, 'revolutionary means'. Such revolutionary attitudes help to explain why the Allies continued to intervene in Russia after the defeat of Germany. The impact of that intervention intensified the attitudes that had, in part, provoked it. The Soviets were left with a feeling of isolation and vulnerability which for years was to dominate their policy towards the hostile, capitalist world into which they had intruded.[25]

Although the intervention failed to unseat the Bolsheviks it did help to prevent the spread of their revolution to the rest of Europe. By the time the last interventionist troops sailed away Lenin realized that his first priority was to ensure the survival of the revolution in Russia itself. In the spring of 1921 he introduced a New Economic Policy which his critics saw as a retreat from socialism. Lenin argued that if he did not make concessions to the peasants they would overthrow the revolution. Change on the domestic front inevitably involved a reassessment of the Soviet attitude to international relations: '. . . a foreign policy of concilia-tion and compromise with the capitalist world was a natural corol-lary of NEP.'[26] We may well wonder why Lenin, the scourge of the capitalists in 1919, was prepared to conciliate them two years later. Carr's resolution of the paradox is of the utmost importance. It helps to explain not only the changed character of Soviet foreign policy after 1921 but also the policies pursued by Stalin during and after the Second World War.

'The change of front', says Carr, 'carried out by Moscow in March 1921 affected the climate in which Soviet foreign policy henceforth operated rather than the substance of that policy. It did not mean, in domestic affairs, the abandonment of the goal of socialism and Communism, or, in foreign affairs, of the goal of world revolution. But it meant a recognition of the necessity of a certain postponement in reaching these goals, and in the meanwhile of building up the economic and diplomatic strength of Soviet Russia by all practicable means, even if these means were in appear-ance a retreat from the direct path to socialism and world revolu-tion. The new foreign policy had been adopted, in the words used by Lenin of NEP, "seriously and for a long time".'[27] How long the policy lasted and to what extent the means seemed to become more important than the ends are questions to be examined later.

One of the earliest results of the new policy was a closer relation-ship between the Soviet Union and Germany. In 1922 at Rapallo they signed a treaty of mutual friendship. Chicherin, the Soviet Foreign Minister, had pointed out that 'in the present period of history, which permits the parallel existence of the old social order and of the new order now being born, economic collaboration between the states representing these two systems of property is imperatively necessary for the general economic reconstruction'.[28] The desire for more normal relations with other states was reflected in the growth of trade between the Soviet Union and a number of capitalist countries, not only with Germany but also with Britain and the United States.[29] That, however, was only one aspect of Western–Soviet relations. Limited economic co-operation did not dispel fundamental distrust. In the opinion of Carr: '. . . Rapallo established the principle that the capitalist world must be prevented at all costs from uniting against the Soviet power and that this could be achieved by proffering the hand of friendship to one of the camps into which that world was divided; and since, throughout the Weimar period, Germany was the weaker of the two groups, this established a special relation between Soviet Russia and Germany.'[30]

We might at this point take firm hold of the fact that the overriding aim of Soviet policy was to safeguard Russia from the designs of all other powers. It can act as a lifeline to help us through the murky waters of the 1930s. In Europe that miserable decade was dominated by Hitler. He re-created the menace of a militarized and expansionist German state. That put the other European powers into a quandary which he deftly turned to his own advantage. They were all uneasy about Nazism but neither the Western democracies nor the Soviet Union wanted to risk war. Hitler, counting on their caution, himself took a number of successful risks. In 1935 he breached the Versailles Treaty by openly re-arming Germany. The British signed a naval convention with him which simply accepted the fact of German re-armament. The League of Nations, which Russia had joined in 1934, took no action. Mutual assistance pacts agreed by France, Czechoslovakia and the Soviet Union were evidence of apprehension about Hitler's intentions. Nevertheless, his gamble succeeded.

Other gambles were equally successful. In 1936 he occupied the demilitarized zone of the Rhineland and in March 1938 forced a union with Austria. He then demanded the cession to Germany of the Sudetenland, a part of Czechoslovakia with a largely German-speaking population. This new move created a major European crisis.

On the face of it there was an obvious antidote to the Nazi threat. The French and the Russians could honour their pact with the Czechs. Hitler would then be forced to climb down or be

The men of Munich: in the front row from left to right Chamberlain, Daladier, Hitler, Mussolini and Ciano, the Italian Foreign Minister.

overwhelmed by superior forces. Unfortunately, the French lacked the will to fight. The appeasement policy of the British Cabinet encouraged their lack of resolve. Their irresolution, in turn, buttressed Chamberlain's decision to give in to Hitler. As a British official observed at the time: 'Outstanding factor is now this peace at any price French attitude which of course lets HMG [the British Government] out and should facilitate a settlement – at the expense of Czechoslovakia. Not very pretty!'[31]

The settlement was reached at Munich on 29 September 1938, when Chamberlain, Daladier (the French Premier), Hitler and Mussolini agreed that the Sudetenland should be ceded to Germany. Benes, the Czech President, acquiesced, despite the impassioned opposition of some of his General Staff,[32] in the dismemberment of his country. The Russians, who had apparently been ready to fight provided that the French also intervened,[33] considered that they, like the Czechs, had been betrayed. They felt that the British and the French had done a deal with Hitler to channel aggression away from themselves. In the words of one Soviet historian: 'The question naturally arises – why did Chamberlain and Daladier so consistently help Hitler to realize his aims, without considering the political disadvantages to their own countries' national interests? Analysis of all the factors involved makes only one answer possible – the Governments of Great Britain and France wanted to direct German aggression towards the east, to satisfy Hitler's claims at the expense of the East European countries . . . they . . . counted on involving Germany and Russia in conflict, thus weakening them both.'[34]

Of course the British and the French governments presented the situation in a very different light. In general they felt that resistance to Hitler would provoke him into declaring war and they were fearful of the consequences of a modern war and the wholesale use of weapons of mass destruction. Exaggerated estimates of the destructive power of bombers were current at that time. The British public were warned that 'the bomber will always get through'. The Western leaders decided that the only way to avoid disaster was to compel the Czechs to give in to Hitler. They discounted suggestions that the Soviet Union could tip the balance against Germany. Lord Butler, then a junior minister at the Foreign Office, has recently commented: 'I was left in no doubt that the Russians themselves did not mean business.'[35] He went on to say that the Rumanians and the Poles had refused to allow Russian troops to cross their territory, thus making effective ground support for the Czechs virtually impossible. Furthermore, 'the great purges [of the Red Army] of 1937 had had a disastrous effect on [its] morale and efficiency'.[36]

Maisky, rebutting those charges, has argued that the Russians did mean business and that '. . . the USSR throughout the whole Munich drama withstood the test with honour'.[37] The debate about Russian preparedness and their intentions in 1938 continues. Naturally, Maisky did not mention that '. . . while . . . promoting through every possible channel the policy of collective security against Nazi Germany, Stalin was during the years 1934 to 1937 seeking in greatest secrecy to negotiate an agreement with Hitler and was rebuffed'.[38] The callous disregard of the Czechoslovaks by the British and the French was paralleled by the two-facedness of the Soviets both before and after the Munich episode.

The settlement at Munich did briefly remove the threat of war: Chamberlain claimed that it had ensured 'peace in our time'. The peace did not last. In March 1939 Hitler occupied the rump of Czechoslovakia and by the summer he was threatening Poland.

Despite the failure of the previous year it seemed imperative for the British, the French and the Russians to agree on some way of stopping him. During the summer of 1939 representatives of the three powers met to work out a course of action. Talks were still going on when news reached London on 21 August that Germany and the Soviet Union were about to make a pact of non-aggression.* Two days later the Nazi–Soviet Pact was signed.

It was a bombshell. Many people in the West had all their suspicions about Soviet intentions confirmed. One British Member of Parliament complained about the 'double-dyed treachery of the Kremlin.'[39] According to Chamberlain, the British had been negotiating in good faith; their military mission in fact was in Moscow when the Soviets did a complete turn about. Their deal with Hitler gave him the green light to attack Poland and so start the Second World War. It was, according to Western opinion, a great betrayal.

The Soviets claimed that they had acted to avoid a betrayal by the West. 'The course taken by the talks . . . showed that the Anglo–French side did not wish to discuss definite military plans, the conditions for allowing Soviet troops to traverse Polish and Rumanian territory, the number of divisions to be committed and so on. The talks arrived at an impasse when Poland announced that she would not allow Soviet troops to cross her territory.'[40] The experience of Munich, so the argument went, had taught the Soviets not to trust the West and they feared that once again Chamberlain was ready to come to terms, behind their backs, with Hitler. Thus to protect themselves they decided to accept the German offer of a non-aggression pact.

Only the small Western Communist Parties accepted the Russian line. They alone were able to convince themselves that the Soviet seizure of Polish lands after the war started was an act of self-defence. Only the same people accepted the same excuse when, in November 1939, the USSR invaded Finland. Roosevelt, the American President, condemned that action in the name of 'all peaceloving peoples'. The British and French governments even considered intervening on behalf of the Finns and in December the USSR was expelled from the League of Nations.[41]

There was a certain irony in the situation. The Soviets had joined

* The British had been remarkably offhand in their conduct of the negotiations. See Taylor, *The Origins of the Second World War* (Penguin) pp. 282–4 and Werth, *Russia at War* (Pan Books) pp. 49–60.

the League of Nations because they sought, in collective security, a safeguard against aggression. They had become disillusioned because the Western powers, so prompt in condemning the USSR in 1939, had previously been totally ineffective against the Fascists. The League's half-hearted sanctions had failed to prevent Mussolini's seizure of Abyssinia. During the Spanish Civil War the British and French politicians had abetted the defeat of the republican government by their dubious policy of non-intervention. A. J. P. Taylor has pointed out that: 'British and French policy . . . decided the outcome of the Spanish civil war. The republic had greater resources, greater popular backing. It could win if it received the correct treatment to which it was entitled by international law: foreign arms for the legitimate government, none for the rebels . . . The rebels had a chance only if they received foreign aid, while the republic received none or very little; and this extraordinary arrangement was provided, though not deliberately, by London and Paris.'★ The arrangement seemed deliberate enough to Stalin.

★ A. J. P. Taylor, *The Origins of the Second World War* p. 157 (Penguin).

The Nazi–Soviet Pact: a Western view of the partition of Eastern Europe.

Taylor himself concedes that British policy 'made sense in Moscow only on the assumption that it desired the triumph of Fascism. The British had allowed Hitler to rearm and to destroy the system of security; they were helping Franco to win in Spain. Soon, surely, they would stand approvingly by while Hitler attacked Soviet Russia; or maybe even cooperate in the enterprise.'★ However, as a result of the Nazi–Soviet Pact, it was the Soviets who stood by while Hitler attacked the West.

Thus, at the end of 1939, Russia was, in Western eyes, as much a pariah as it had been during the wars of intervention. The Soviet Communists had shown themselves to be unscrupulous double-dealers. The very people who had denounced Hitler so vehemently now sheltered behind a non-aggression pact, leaving the British and French to stand up to the Nazis. For their part, the Russians were thankful that their great leader and teacher, Stalin, had outwitted the schemers of London and Paris who had hoped to embroil them in a bloody war with Germany. These attitudes persisted until the Russians did get involved in the war, when Hitler invaded them.

★ Ibid, p. 162.

Two

STRESSES IN THE GRAND ALLIANCE

On 18 December 1940 Hitler issued his directive for Operation Barbarossa, his plan to push Soviet Russia back beyond a line from Archangel in the north to the River Volga in the south. At dawn on 22 June 1941 the great offensive began. After a fierce artillery bombardment and a series of air strikes which destroyed a large part of the Soviet Air Force on the ground, forward units of the Wehrmacht opened the way for an army of three million men who attacked on a front 1,250 miles long. They advanced at a remarkable rate. So complete was the Nazi success that many official observers in Britain reckoned that within a couple of months the Russians would be forced to admit defeat.[1]

Even so, Churchill immediately offered to help them. In a broadcast on the evening of the invasion he declared that, while he would not retract any of the criticisms he had made of the Communist system, he was ready to ally himself with anyone who was fighting the Nazis. To his secretary he remarked: 'If Hitler invaded Hell I would make at least a favourable reference to the Devil in the House of Commons.'[2] Roosevelt followed suit and sent a representative to Moscow to arrange American assistance. Thus Hitler's triumphs created an understanding between the two principal capitalist powers and the USSR.

Roosevelt's appreciation that the Soviets were in effect fighting America's fight was not shared by all Americans. Truman, who was to succeed him as President, had a very different approach. In a speech in July 1941 he said: 'If we see that Germany is winning the war we ought to help Russia, and if Russia is winning we ought to help Germany, and in that way let them kill as many as possible.'[3] That was the authentic voice of many Americans who hated Communism and saw no good reason for giving up their isolationist attitudes. Circumstances, however, forced all Americans to accept what many of them felt was an unholy alliance. On 7 December 1941 the Japanese bombed the US naval base at Pearl

Harbor, thus in effect declaring war. In support of his Japanese allies Hitler also declared war and so committed Germany to fighting the world's greatest industrial power.

Hitler was no fool and for a time it did seem that the Axis powers might be triumphant. Indeed a year was to pass before, in Churchill's phrase, the tide turned. Three decisive victories for the Allies marked the end of Axis expansion. Midway, El Alamein and Stalingrad presaged the final defeat of Germany and Japan (the Italians, despite the posturings of Mussolini, scarcely counted). The war still had a long way to run and millions were still to die but by 1943 the Allied leaders could start considering the post-war settlement.

Churchill was preoccupied with preserving the power of the British Empire and Commonwealth. Traditionally, British policy was to prevent any single power dominating Europe. Essentially a traditionalist and an enemy of Communism, Churchill was bound to resist any extension of Soviet influence beyond Russia's pre-war boundaries. During a visit to Washington in May 1943 he had commented that it 'was important to re-create a strong France; for the prospect of having no strong country on the map between

The ruins of Stalingrad in flames: the epitome of Russian suffering and resistance.

England and Russia was not attractive'. He also felt that 'it would be necessary for the United States to be associated in some way with the policing of Europe, in which Great Britain would obviously also have to take part'.[4]

Stalin was concerned, above all, with the security of the Soviet Union. It might be objected that he had a much wider aim – to make the whole world Communist. His past record, however, had shown him to be primarily concerned with Russian interests. In the words of one historian: ' "Socialism in one country" was perhaps the only one of Stalin's policies which involved a deep and personal commitment. It meant that diplomatic activity in European affairs was mainly designed to keep Europe as far away from the Soviet Union as possible. Now, on 22 June 1941, the whole scheme was shattered in an instant. Russia was to be firmly involved in Europe and its problems. All possibility of manoeuvre and manipulation had gone; overnight the Soviet Union had necessarily become the client of its new allies, Britain and then the United States.'[5]

Stalin did not care to be anyone's client. As before, he wanted the freedom to develop Russian in his way. He recognized that the Red Army could push Russia's frontiers farther West, that as it advanced the USSR was becoming involved firmly in Europe. But a new frontier of Russian influence did not necessarily entail a policy that was very different from the one before the war. 'In practice he returned to the same dual form of international policy which he had evolved before the war; the pursuit of Soviet interests abroad which co-ordinated both Soviet diplomacy and organized communism into one coherent instrument. No risks were to be taken in the pursuit of impossible revolutionary tasks.'[6]

We consider later whether that judgment was borne out by the facts. Now we examine briefly the policy of the third ally, the USA. Both the British and the Russians had some specific objectives in mind. The same could hardly be said of the Americans. The United States had been forced into war in December 1941 by Japan and Germany. Their immediate aim was to restore the *status quo* by defeating those who sought to change it. This was 'a task of staggering proportions but one that carried with it great opportunities for the extension of American power and influence. The United States was quick to grasp them.'[7] Roosevelt was no doubt confident that American influence would play an important part in the eventual peace settlement. But he had no clear picture of the kind of settlement he wanted. In January 1943 he declared that Anglo–American policy towards Germany and Japan (and by implication Italy) was to demand unconditional surrender. Presumably this would be followed by a period of military occupation. What would follow that was unclear. As the New Deal showed, Roosevelt was essentially a pragmatist. He preferred to play by ear rather than follow a set score. His attitude was that post-war problems were best settled after the war was over. He wished to concentrate on winning it and avoid bickering over war aims. This was not always possible. Both Churchill and Stalin were anxious to settle some political issues while the war was in progress.

One issue which demonstrated the difficulty of arranging a peace settlement acceptable to all the Allies was the fate of Poland. The British had officially gone to war to defend Polish independence. They were thus concerned that at the end of the war Poland should recover its lost territories and have an independent government. The Russians were no less interested in Poland. It was their experience that the Polish plains were a well-worn path for Western invaders of Russia. After their deal with Hitler in 1939 they had taken over a large part of Eastern Poland. Once they regained it from the Nazis they did not intend to give it up but were prepared to see the Poles get compensation in the West by taking over territory from Germany. They were not prepared to see an unfriendly government in charge of post-war Poland. (It may be recalled that the anti-Bolshevik pre-war government had undermined attempts to organize collective security against Hitler.) In Stalin's view, Poland could have any government it liked, provided that it was acceptable to him.

The Big Three met at Teheran in November 1943 and, in the main, agreed on the boundaries of Poland. The USSR was to keep almost all the Eastern part. Poland was to be compensated, at Germany's expense, by the acquisition of much of East Prussia, Danzig, Pomerania and Silesia up to the Oder and Neisse rivers. The problem of which government would rule in Poland remained unsettled. Britain and the USA favoured the Provisional Government which had been set up in London. The Soviets distrusted the London Poles, who were unwilling to give up the Eastern lands, and encouraged another group, the Union of Polish Patriots, which was based in Russia. While the Union did not claim to be a government itself, it was highly critical of the London group and felt that the future government of Poland must come from the people in Poland, not from the émigrés.

Behind the immediate difficulties was the age-old hostility between Poles and Russians, which had existed well before the Bolshevik Revolution. It had merely been exacerbated by the addition of anti-Communism to the old feeling of anti-Russianism. Recent incidents fed that hatred. In April 1943 German troops in occupied Russia claimed to have found a mass grave in Katyn Forest near the city of Smolensk, in which the bodies of several thousand Polish Army officers, who had been taken prisoner by the Russians in 1939, were buried. The Nazis made a great deal of propaganda by claiming that the officers had been murdered by the Russians. Of course, the Soviets denied responsibility and counter-claimed that it had been a German atrocity. However, many Poles suspected, and with good reason, that the Russians had, in fact, been guilty.[8]

Another event which inflamed relations between the London Poles and the Russians, and between Churchill and Stalin, was the Warsaw Rising of 1944. On 1 August Poles under the command of leaders who supported the government in exile in London, rose against the Nazi garrison. The uprising came as a complete surprise to the Russians, who had been halted in their advance just across the River Vistula from Warsaw. Despite heroic efforts, the Poles were crushed by the Germans who killed some 300,000 people, most of them civilians. They also razed Warsaw to the ground. Westerners were horrified by the callousness, in their view, of the Russians in refusing to give any help to the resistance fighters. Stalin argued that determined opposition by the Germans made it impossible to force a crossing of the Vistula in order to rescue Warsaw. On strategic grounds there appear to have been good reasons for the Russian attitude.[9] However, it is almost impossible to understand why they would not allow the Western Allies the use of Russian-controlled airfields to drop supplies to the beleaguered Poles. In the opinion of Deutscher: 'The tragedy of Warsaw added new bitterness to the anti-Russian feeling in Poland, and it shocked even Stalin's admirers in the West. It is difficult to think what political calculation, be it even the most cynical one, accounted for his attitude. He was moved by that unscrupulous rancour and insensible spite of which he had given so much proof during the great purges.'[10]

Outraged though he was, Churchill visited Moscow in October 1944 – the month when Warsaw was almost wiped off the map – and made a secret agreement with Stalin about the spheres of influence in the Balkans of Britain and Russia.[11] On his return to London he stressed in the House of Commons his resolve that Poland should be restored and should be allowed to 'model her social institutions . . . in any way her people choose, provided . . . that these are not on fascist lines, and provided that Poland stands loyally as a barrier and friend of Russia . . .'[12] Thus he openly endorsed Stalin's policy that only a government friendly to the Soviets would be acceptable in Poland. In the light of the ancient enmity and of the Katyn and Warsaw episodes it seemed that only the Polish Communists would fit the bill. Despite all Churchill's promptings, the London Poles would not dismiss those members of the government who were bitterly anti-Soviet, nor would they accept Russian claims to the Polish lands they had seized in 1939.

In January 1945 Stalin recognized the Communist-dominated Lublin Committee as the legitimate government of Poland. There were then two Polish governments, one in London and another in Poland. A meeting of the three Allied leaders was arranged to put an end to that impossible situation. As Churchill later remarked: 'Poland had indeed been the most urgent reason for the Yalta Conferences.'[13] Yalta was one of the great wartime conferences where a number of important problems were tackled.[14] Here we are concerned primarily with the Polish question which was perhaps the most crucial, especially since the way it was settled helped to determine the fate of the whole of Eastern Europe. It was only after prolonged discussions that a solution of some sort emerged. Eventually Roosevelt and Churchill agreed that the Lublin Committee should provide the nucleus of a new Polish government. Stalin, in return, guaranteed to include in the government representatives of the London Poles. He also agreed to hold 'free and unfettered elections as soon as possible on the basis of universal suffrage and secret ballot'.

The immediate Western reaction to the conference was hopeful. On 27 February 1945 Churchill informed the House of Commons: 'The impression I brought back . . . is that Marshal Stalin and the Soviet leaders wish to live in honourable friendship and equity with the Western democracies. I feel also that their word is their bond.'[15] This mood was short-lived. Soon it appeared that Yalta was 'the watershed between wartime co-operation and the opening sorties of the post-war era – "the Cold War" '.[16] Indeed we can hardly follow the unfolding of the Cold War unless we consider the various ways in which Yalta has been interpreted.

A common view is that it was a major diplomatic triumph for the Soviets. Thus Donnelly comments: 'The significant fact from Stalin's point of view was that he had conceded nothing . . . that could not be ignored or circumnavigated when the appropriate time came.'[17] In other words, Stalin was playing on the gullibility of the West, giving merely paper promises, as a previous dictator had at Munich. 'The American attempt to play the good neighbour failed for the same reason as did Neville Chamberlain's policy of being a good neighbour to Hitler and Mussolini. Dictatorships are never appeased.'[18] Note how Donnelly equates Stalin with Hitler and raises the spectre of appeasement. This was soon to become the orthodox view among American policy makers.

Stettinius, Roosevelt's Secretary of State, while accepting the

The Big Three: Churchill, Roosevelt and Stalin at the Yalta Conference, February 1945.

point about Stalin's untrustworthiness, argues that Yalta was a fair settlement. 'As a result of the military situation, it was not a question of what Great Britain and the United States would permit Russia to do in Poland, but what the two countries could persuade the Soviet Union to accept . . . Poland and most of Eastern Europe . . . was in the hands of the Red Army.' Nevertheless, Stettinius contends that 'the Yalta Agreements were, on the whole a diplomatic triumph for the United States and Great Britain. The real difficulties with the Soviet Union came *after* Yalta when the agreements were not respected.'[19]

Yet another interpretation contests the views both of Donnelly and Stettinius. According to Clemens there was no 'good neighbour policy'. 'The undoing of the Soviet Union's favourable situation in Poland . . . remained an underlying goal of Anglo–American diplomacy.'[20] Such a goal was unlikely to be achieved while the Red Army remained in Poland. However, Clemens argues, the fact that Stalin had military control of Poland did not necessarily mean that his guarantee of free elections was an empty formula. 'As to free elections,' she says, 'there was no reason to believe that Stalin – whose record included sponsoring free elections in Finland and Austria, backing the West's rightist régimes in France, Italy and Belgium, and supporting Churchill's free hand in Greece against the powerful leftists – would not allow moderately free elections in Poland as promised. But when Western hostility threatened everything short of war with the Soviet Union, the Russians increasingly abandoned free elections and co-operation in favour of consolidation of a defensive perimeter* in Eastern Europe.'[21]

Confronted by such divergent views of Yalta, how are we to decide which is the most realistic? It is clear enough that Stalin could be trusted only to serve the ends of the Soviet Union. On that basis we may tend to accept Donnelly's version. However, the fact that Stalin was unscrupulously pro-Russian does not invalidate the contention that Western leaders were calculatingly anti-Soviet. We have seen that both Churchill and Stettinius considered that there had been a reasonable settlement at Yalta. It might be helpful now to examine how, after Yalta, relations between the Soviets and the West began to deteriorate.

The crucial event in the immediate post-Yalta period was the

---

* It was hardly surprising that Stalin was determined to consolidate a defensive perimeter. Twenty million Russians had died in the course of the war.

death of Roosevelt on 12 April 1945. During his long presidency FDR had made many enemies. After his death they accused him of being a dupe of the Communists. They denounced his New Deal as socialistic, although it was obvious to all bar political illiterates that, by liberalizing the capitalist system in the USA, FDR had helped to preserve it. Roosevelt was no socialist. He had, however, been prepared to recognize Soviet interests and to negotiate with Stalin. Just before he died he had resisted pressure from Churchill to take a stronger stand on Poland. 'I would', he had said, 'minimize the general Soviet problem as much as possible because these problems . . . seem to arise every day and most of them straighten out . . .'[22]

Truman, who succeeded Roosevelt, had a different approach.[23] Soon after becoming President he told Harriman, the ambassador to Russia, that he was 'not afraid of the Russians' and that 'the Russians needed us more than we needed them'.[24] He would make as few concessions as possible. While he did not expect to get 'one hundred percent of what we proposed', he felt that 'we should be able to get eighty-five percent'.[25] He assumed that the Russians needed American money and would therefore be forced to concede most American demands. Thus he berated the Soviet Foreign Minister, while he was in Washington, about the Polish question. After shouting at Molotov 'in the language of a Missouri mule driver', Truman told him that Stalin must reorganize the Polish government by including some of the London Poles and must also hold elections. When Molotov protested that he had never been spoken to like that before he was curtly informed that if he carried out his agreements he would not 'get talked to like that'.[26]

'From the eminence of eleven days in power', comments Fleming, 'Harry Truman made his decision to lay down the law to an ally which had contributed more in blood and agony to the common cause than we had – and about Poland, an area through which the Soviet Union had been invaded three times since 1914 . . . the basis for the Cold War was laid on 23 April in the scourging which Truman administered to Molotov, giving notice that in areas of the most crucial concern to Russia our wishes must be obeyed.'[27]

Clemens suggests that, on this occasion, the President was setting American policy on a new tack. 'Truman', she says, 'set out to implement the Yalta agreements by changing them . . . He handed him [Molotov] a memorandum which equated fulfillment of the Yalta decisions with the establishment of a "new" government. As we have previously seen, at Yalta the United States had agreed in writing to a "reorganized" version of the Polish Provisional Government "which is now functioning in Poland". Stalin noted the new direction of Truman's policy with some alarm . . .'[28]

On 24 April he wrote to Truman pointing out that: 'Poland borders on the Soviet Union which cannot be said about Great Britain or the USA. . . . I do not know whether a genuinely representative Government has been established in Greece, or whether the Belgian Government is a genuinely democratic one. The Soviet Union was not consulted when those Governments were being formed, nor did it claim the right to interfere in those matters, because it realizes how important Belgium and Greece are to the security of Great Britain. . . . You evidently do not agree that the Soviet Union is entitled to seek in Poland a Government that would be friendly to it, that the Soviet Government cannot agree to the existence in Poland of a Government hostile to it. To put it plainly, you want me to renounce the interests of the security of the Soviet Union; but I cannot proceed against the interests of my country.'[29]

The crucial question was whether the interests of the Soviet Union could be reconciled with those of the United States. To answer that question we must try to discover what those interests were.

Three

THE COLD WAR BEGINS

In 1917 Woodrow Wilson had invited the American people to join a crusade against German militarism. In 1941 Roosevelt recruited them for another crusade against Nazi tyranny and the warlords of Japan. On both occasions US policy was presented as an idealistic struggle for a better world. Wilson's emphasis on the League of Nations and FDR's concern for the United Nations Organization seemed to support this view. In the words of McNeill: 'Just as the expansion and consolidation of Russian state power at home and abroad had, since the Bolshevik Revolution, drawn strength and justification from Marxian doctrine, so the expansion and consolidation of American power seemed to have found an intellectual – or if you will, verbal – justification in the myths associated with the names of Wilson and Roosevelt. Peace, justice, freedom and plenty, if one believes them attainable, are powerful and positive goals for which to strive; goals which may sustain an active foreign policy and lead to actions in places where national self-interest alone would never venture.'[1] Important though such myths are they do not adequately explain the motives of America's leaders. They omit the element of self-interest in Wilson's conception of liberal nationalism.[2] They also ignore the concern for economic issues that influenced Roosevelt and his successors.

Commenting on the importance of economic factors, Ambrose asserts: 'American foreign policy in the crucial years from 1945 to 1950 can be understood only in reference to the widespread fear of another depression.'[3] To avoid such a depression American leaders were determined to secure foreign markets. The Second World War had opened up great opportunities for the Americans to bring about the kind of politico-economic order that Woodrow Wilson had envisaged after the First World War. They felt they had the power to insist on an open door everywhere. The markets of all nations would lie open to American goods and US business interests could be established throughout the world. Truman argued indeed that only when the world had been converted to the American way of life would the US be secure. Although Truman and other leaders justified their policies in moral terms, and did genuinely believe that what was good for America was good for the world, their primary objective was of course the security, prosperity and prestige (even the dominance) of the United States. There was a discernible gap between the altruistic myths and the reality.[4]

Soviet foreign policy displays a similar divergence of fact from theory. Soviet state power has, in McNeill's phrase, 'drawn strength and justification' from Marxism.[5] Russian leaders have claimed to be seeking 'peace, justice, freedom and plenty' by following the road to world Communism. However, even in the early stages of their journey, they were soon stressing the need to build up the 'economic and diplomatic strength of Soviet Russia'.[6] Time and again the interests of the Soviet Union were placed above the cause of world revolution. The justification for such a policy was that Russia was the only Communist country in a hostile capitalist world. If it succumbed to its enemies there would be no base from which to launch other revolutions. The implication was that when the Soviet Union was impregnable, its leaders would advance from building socialism in one country to spread Communism throughout the world.

By May 1945 the Red Army had occupied most of Eastern Europe, Nazi Germany was crushed and Japan was on its last legs. It might appear, therefore, that the Soviet Union was finally secure enough to put world revolution first on its agenda. That was certainly the fear of some Western leaders. Even in August 1944, Churchill had exclaimed to his doctor and confidant, Moran: 'Good God, can't you see that the Russians are spreading across Europe like a tide.'[7] As the war in Europe neared its end 'he had ordered Montgomery to keep German arms intact, in case they had to be used against the Russians'.[8] Some later historians have taken a very different view, arguing that the Soviet Union, though victorious, had been weakened by the war and was still primarily concerned with defending its gains, rather than with mounting a revolutionary offensive.

Kolko, for example, states: 'More aware than anyone else of their own weaknesses in the event of a conflict with the United States, the Russians pursued a conservative and cautious line wherever they could find local non-Communist groups willing to abjure the traditional diplomacy of the cordon sanitaire and anti-Bolshevism . . . they showed neither more nor less respect for an unborn functional democracy in Eastern Europe than the Americans and British evidenced in Italy, Greece or Belgium. For neither the Americans, British nor Russians were willing to permit democracy to run its course anywhere in Europe at the cost of damaging their vital strategic and economic interests . . . The Russians had no intention of Bolshevizing Eastern Europe in 1945 if . . . they could find alternatives.'9

It is evident by now that the objectives of the United States and the Soviet Union are open to several different interpretations. Different observers give their own twist to the kaleidoscope and create their own patterns. We begin to appreciate that, though a particular pattern may seem clear enough, the materials can be re-arranged to make a number of other pictures. Fulbright has pointed out that: 'The motives of Soviet policy . . . are a synthesis of ideological conviction, historical conditioning, rational calculation, irrational fears and hopes, and personal predilictions – which is to say they are obscure.'10 The same could be said about American policy. This preliminary examination of US and Soviet motives

Still allies: American and Russian troops arm in arm at their meeting point in Germany, April 1945.

will have served its purpose if it warns us against those who seek to oversimplify them.

As we return to the narrative, one simple point can be made: that after Yalta the Grand Alliance was being strained. Differences that had been played down during the war became more and more evident as the war drew to a close. The hope that the United Nations Organization would help to resolve the differences was short-lived. Even at the San Francisco conference the Soviet Union and the USA clashed on a number of issues. At one point the influential Senator Vandenberg even welcomed the prospect of Russia's withdrawing from the conference.[11] In fact the Russians remained and became founder members of the new international body. It was soon evident however, that the UNO was dominated by the United States and could not act as a genuine arbiter in the struggle that was developing between the Americans and the Russians.[12]

Shortly after the San Francisco conference dispersed the war in Europe ended (May 1945) with the unconditional surrender of Germany and its allies. The war in Asia continued but Japan was isolated and her defeat imminent. Before the Japanese too capitulated there was another meeting of the leaders of the Grand Alliance at Potsdam. Several important decisions were taken at the conference, which lasted from 17 July to 2 August.[13] A Council of the Foreign Ministers of the major powers was established to draw up peace treaties with the defeated nations. It was agreed that Germany must be demilitarized, denazified and democratized. After lengthy discussions a formula for reparations payments was produced. Each occupying power was authorized to remove property from its own zone of Germany and to take over German assets in areas outside Germany. A control council, consisting of representatives of the occupying powers – the US, Russia, Britain and France – was to decide matters affecting Germany as a whole.

The agreements barely concealed a lack of trust among the powers. The provision that each of them should deal with reparations in its own zone was necessary because they could not agree on a common policy for the whole country. The point on which they did concur, that Germany should be kept under military occupation, was bound to cause friction. Deutscher has remarked that it 'was enough to drive the policies of the Allies in opposite directions. The longer they were to stay on performing the functions of a German government . . . the more would each occupying power be inclined to mould in its own image the economic and political life of its part of Germany . . . It was as unnatural for the officers of the Soviet military administration to administer a capitalist economy in eastern Germany as it was for their counterparts of the American military government to reorganize western Germany on socialist lines.'[14]

At Potsdam the powers quarrelled about their spheres of influence elsewhere in Europe. The West accused the Russians of refusing to hold free elections in Bulgaria and Rumania. They countercharged that the British were rigging elections in Greece for the benefit of a reactionary monarchy; they also claimed that the West had set up an 'Italian Fascist' régime in Trieste.

The impact of the disputes at Potsdam on President Truman was startling. He records in his memoirs: 'The persistent way in which Stalin blocked one of the war preventative measures I had proposed showed how his mind worked and what he was after. I had proposed the internationalization of all the principal waterways. [According to the British interpreter at Potsdam, "a remarkable though hardly practical idea".[15]] Stalin did not want this. What Stalin wanted was control of the Black Sea Straits and the Danube.

The New Big Three: Attlee, Truman and Stalin at Potsdam. In the back row, left to right, Admiral Leahy, Bevin, Byrnes and Molotov.

The Russians were planning world conquest.'[16] It apparently did not occur to the President that Stalin might be resisting the internationalization of the waterways in order to make it more difficult for the American commercial interests to penetrate into Eastern Europe. The notion of Stalin's playing a defensive role was for Truman unthinkable. 'Hitler was hardly in his grave; already Truman had substituted Stalin for Hitler as the madman who had to be stopped. The tone of the Cold War was established.'[17]

It might well appear that the most important effect of the Potsdam Conference was its influence on the attitudes of President Truman.[18] That certainly was Truman's own view: 'As I left for home, I felt that we had achieved several important agreements. But more important were some of the conclusions I had reached in my own mind and a realization of what I had to do in shaping future foreign policy.'[19]

Truman had good reason to feel that he could shape a policy to suit America's needs: that, for example, he could stop Stalin. While at Potsdam he had received news of the successful testing of the atomic bomb. Churchill later commented on that news: 'We were in the presence of a new factor in human affairs . . . We possessed powers which were irresistible . . . our outlook on the future was transformed.'[20] It was ironical that Truman had gone to Potsdam partly to ensure Russian participation in the war against Japan. The new bomb had completely changed the situation. As Churchill said: '. . . we should not need the Russians.'[21] At Potsdam Truman had authorized the dropping of the bomb on Japan. On his way home he was informed of the devastation of Hiroshima. 'This', he said, 'is the greatest thing in history!'[22]

Much has been written about the decision to drop the bombs on Hiroshima and Nagasaki. Fleming has pointed out: 'In midsummer 1945 four powerful urges pushed our leaders toward the swift use of the atomic bomb: (1) to save American lives; (2) to shorten the war; (3) to announce the atomic age fittingly; and (4) to minimize the expansion of Russian power in the Far East. In the earlier stages of the decision the first two motives were the strongest; in the final stages the last two appear to have become decisive.'[23]

Alperovitz has examined in detail the military reasons for Truman's decision. He notes that: '. . . *before the atomic bomb was dropped each of the Joint Chiefs of Staff advised that it was highly likely that Japan could be forced to surrender "unconditionally", without the use of the bomb and without an invasion.*'[24] [His italics.] In support of their view he quotes the US Strategic Bombing Survey: 'The Survey's conclusion is unequivocal: "Japan would have surrendered even if the atomic bombs had not been dropped, even if Russia had not entered the war, and even if no invasion had been planned or contemplated." '[25] He concludes that the decision was determined by political objectives: 'The evidence strongly suggests that the view which the President's personal representative offered to one of the atomic scientists in May 1945 was an accurate statement of policy: "Mr Byrnes did not argue that it was necessary to use the bomb against the cities of Japan in order to win the war ...Mr Byrnes's ... view was that our possessing and demonstrating the bomb would make Russia more manageable in Europe ..." '[26] This accords with the opinion Blackett expressed in 1948, 'that the dropping of the atomic bombs was not so much the last military act of the Second World War, as the first act of the cold diplomatic war with Russia now in progress.'[27]

The American leaders certainly believed that it had strengthened their bargaining power. Even before the test at Alamogordo, Truman had predicted: 'If it explodes, as I think it will, I'll ... have a hammer on those boys!'[28] [The Russians.] On the very day of the

Hiroshima.

second explosion at Nagasaki, he spoke with a new confidence about Bulgaria and Rumania. 'These nations', he said, 'are not to be the spheres of influence of any one power'.[29] Byrnes, his newly appointed Secretary of State, was also hopeful: 'The bomb might well put us in a position to dictate our own terms. . . .'[30] Truman and his colleagues considered their terms to be wholly reasonable, based, in their view, on agreements already accepted by Stalin. They were all the more determined, therefore, to use their military power to enforce them. It was a policy described by Stimson as wearing 'this weapon rather ostentatiously on our hip'. Its effect on the Russians was, as he later appreciated, to increase 'their suspicions and distrust of our purposes and motives . . .'[31]

Soviet suspicions were well founded. At Potsdam Truman had deliberately concealed from Stalin the existence of the atomic bomb, fobbing him off with vague talk about a new weapon that had been developed.[32] His behaviour after Hiroshima and Nagasaki suggested that, as Khrushchev later commented, he was 'hostile and spiteful toward the Soviet Union'.[33] Within a few months, the *New Times* of Moscow was to declare: 'The atomic bomb is a signal for reactionaries all over the world to agitate for a new crusade against the Soviet Union.'[34] Presumably, Truman intended to make the Soviets apprehensive in order to make them more amenable. As he said in his memoirs: 'Force is the only thing the Russians understand.'[35] That remark epitomizes his inflexibility and the narrowness of his vision. He reduced a complicated international situation to the crude melodrama of a bad western film with himself in the role of a sharp-shooting sheriff.

Stalin, however, refused to play the part of the foiled villain and called Truman's bluff. He acted on the assumption that the atomic bomb was a 'paper tiger', that strategically it could be ignored while tactically it must be taken into account.[36] Thus he put a high priority on the making of a Russian bomb and at the same time refused to be intimidated by the American bombs. Events justified his policy and showed that Truman had been mistaken. As Blackett has said: 'The belief in absolute atomic power did indeed corrupt judgment.'[37] Gradually, however, the flaws in 'this magical theory of defence by a few bombs' became clear. It was recognized that, for example, the American atomic monopoly did not guarantee the safety of Western Europe. A few bombs dropped on Russian cities, in response to a Soviet invasion, could not prevent the Red Army from advancing rapidly beyond the River Elbe. They might have killed hundreds of thousands of Russians but 'would not have hamstrung the Russian war machine'.[38]

In the immediate post-war period the American leaders were not primarily concerned about a possible Soviet threat to Western Europe. Their main objective was to prevent Eastern Europe from remaining within the Soviet sphere. However, the effect of their atomic bombs was to consolidate Soviet control in that area. Walter Lippmann remarked: 'The more we threaten to demolish Russian cities, the more obvious it is that the Russian defence would be to ensconce themselves in European cities which we could not demolish without massacring hundreds of thousands of our own friends.'[39] Fleming underlines that point: 'Up to this time control of Eastern Europe had seemed vital to them as a means of preventing a German come-back. Now the same region was even more vital as a buffer against the atomic-armed West.'[40] Predictably, Truman's toughness had made Stalin more, not less, inflexible. 'He and Molotov continued to do as they pleased, to refuse to hold elections or to allow Western observers to travel freely in Eastern Europe. The region was not opened up to American economic penetration.'[41]

By the end of 1945 there was a gulf of mistrust separating the USA and the Soviet Union. Yet there still seemed to be the faint possibility of bridging it. In December, at a conference in Moscow, the Foreign Ministers did reach agreement on several important points.[42] The procedure for making peace treaties with Germany's satellites was drawn up. There was to be a Soviet/American conference on Korea: the troops of both powers were to be withdrawn from China. The ministers concurred in the establishment of a United Nations Atomic Energy Commission.[43] They also promised to send a three-power commission to Rumania to prepare for free elections. Molotov agreed to add two representatives of democratic groups to the Bulgarian cabinet. Byrnes, for the USA, and Bevin, the British Foreign Minister, promised to recognize the governments of Bulgaria and Rumania in return for the concessions made by the Russians.

To some observers it seemed that 'the impasse among the powers had been broken . . .'[44] Cordell Hull, a former US Secretary of State, noted: 'Understanding, confidence, friendliness, and the whole spirit of international co-operation have greatly improved the work of this conference.'[45] Truman was furious. He complained that Byrnes had 'taken upon himself to move the foreign policy of the United States in a direction to which I would not and could not agree.'[46] He wrote a letter to Byrnes, which he read to him in the Oval Room of the White House on 5 January 1946.

Inter alia he said: 'There isn't a doubt in my mind that Russia intends an invasion of Turkey and the seizure of the Black Sea Straits to the Mediterranean. Unless Russia is faced with an iron fist and strong language another war is in the making. Only one language do they understand – "How many divisions have you?" We should refuse to recognize Bulgaria and Rumania until they comply with our requirements . . . we should maintain complete control over Japan and the Pacific. We should rehabilitate China and create a strong central government there. We should do the same for Korea. Then we should insist on the return of our ships from Russia and force a settlement of the Lend-Lease debt of Russia. I'm tired of babying the Soviets.'[47] In his memoirs he adds a postscript to the letter: 'My memorandum to Byrnes not only clarified the Secretary's position but it was also the point of departure of our policy. "I'm tired of babying the Soviets", I had said, and I meant it.'[48]

'It is a little difficult,' says Fleming, 'to set down the occasions on which we had babied the Russians, but Mr Truman's inability to block the consolidation of their wartime gains seemed like that to him, and there would be no more of it.'[49] Halle, himself a former official of the State Department, has recorded that Truman was not alone in fearing the Russians: '. . . my recollection remains that the predominant worry in Washington, as the war approached its end, was over the deadly struggle to contain the Soviet Union that could already be foreseen.'[50]

The preoccupation of some Americans with the Soviet threat was shown by their reaction to a speech made by Stalin on 9 February 1946. It was critical of the capitalist system and very complimentary to the Red Army. Since it was an election speech, it is hardly surprising that Stalin extolled the strength of the Soviet system, which had enabled Russia to survive the war and would ensure its rapid recovery.[51] In Fleming's opinion 'any belligerent intention in his speech had to be deduced by implication and by somewhat strained interpretation'.[52] Nevertheless, it was seen as 'the turning point in post-war history', and one of the liberal justices of the US Supreme Court called it the 'Declaration of World War Three'.[53]

There was indeed one area where the Russians were, in Truman's phrase, 'on the march' – Iran. Stalin was anxious to acquire some share of Iranian oil, most of which was controlled by Anglo–American companies. He therefore illegally maintained his troops in Iran after the end of the war and supported a revolt in the northern part of the country in order to exert pressure on the Iranian government. Byrnes protested vigorously and, within three weeks, a joint declaration by Iran and the USSR stated that Soviet troops were to be withdrawn and that an Iranian–Soviet oil company would be formed, subject to ratification by the Iranian parliament. The Russians pulled out on 6 May 1946 and the following year the parliament refused to ratify the oil company treaty. To the Americans the incident was evidence that 'the Soviets were bent on world conquest'.[54]

There was, however, another side to the question, which Horowitz has described: 'As the Russians left, the Americans moved in – not with troops and revolution – "but silently with dollars in support of the *status quo*". In addition to American funds, the Iranian Government received American advisers . . . and Iran became in effect "an American satellite" . . . "this 'defense' base that America had for the taking was six thousand miles from America but on Russia's most sensitive border. Russia could legitimately adopt the question the West put to her: where does security end short of domination of the whole earth?" Thereafter, "Russia fought tooth and nail to close her satellite nations to the 'Iranian method'." '[55]

While the Soviet Union was 'throwing its weight around'[56] in Iran, Churchill delivered an openly aggressive speech at Fulton on 5 March 1946. 'From Stettin in the Baltic to Trieste in the Adriatic, an iron curtain has descended across the Continent.' Thus he described the establishment of a Soviet sphere of influence. While rejecting the idea that the Russians wanted another war, he warned: 'What they desire is the fruits of war and the indefinite expansion of their power and doctrines.' To counter this he wanted 'the establishment of conditions of freedom and democracy as rapidly as possible in all countries'. Presumably by 'all countries' he meant those behind as well as those in front of the 'iron curtain'. To achieve such conditions he urged a 'fraternal association' of the

USA and Britain and the 'continuation of the intimate relationship between our military advisers . . .' He explained that those relationships should lead to 'common study of potential dangers, similarity of weapons and manuals of instruction and inter-change of officers and cadets at colleges'. The close military co-operation between the two countries should 'carry with it the continuance of the present facilities for mutual security by the joint use of all naval and air force bases in the possession of either country all over the world'.[57]

As one Russian commented: 'Churchill offered the Americans a military alliance against the Soviet Union.'[58] The correspondent of the *New York Times*, describing the impact of the speech in Russia, reported: 'Moscow received it hysterically, as if the atomic bombs might start dropping before midnight.'[59] Churchill, having been defeated in the general election of July 1945, was speaking as a private individual. But his prestige was still great and his oratorical skill had not diminished. 'His was the first full-length picture of a Red Russia out to conquer the world. Backed by the immense authority of his war record, and by the charm of his great personality, it pre-conditioned many millions of listeners for a giant new cordon sanitaire around Russia, for a developing world crusade to smash world communism in the name of Anglo–Saxon democracy.'[60]

Initially, however, outside the ruling circles, the speech was not well received in America. During the Second World War the American public had been shown the Soviet Union as a gallant ally against the Nazis. At the beginning of 1946 most Americans had had enough of war and were not yet in the mood to maintain their armed forces for a new crusade against their former allies. Most press comment was hostile. The reaction of the *Chicago Sun* was typical: 'To follow the standard raised by this great but blinded aristocrat would be to march to the world's most ghastly war. Let Mr Truman's rejection of the poisonous doctrines declared by Mr Churchill be prompt and emphatic.'[61]

In fact, the speech stated openly what Truman and some of his advisers privately thought. Two days after making it, Churchill sent a telegram to Attlee and Bevin explaining the situation. Truman 'had read a mimeographed copy of the final draft on the train to Fulton . . . "He told me that he thought it was admirable and would do nothing but good though it would make a stir" . . . A copy of the speech had also been shown . . . to Mr Byrnes . . . who was excited by it . . . and to Admiral Leahy [one of Truman's most intimate advisers] who was enthusiastic'.[62]

The Fulton speech 'marked the critical point where relations between the West and the East turned for the worse'.[63] Churchill's call to action provoked extreme reactions from both sides. George Earle, former American Minister to Bulgaria 'urged that Russia be given an ultimatum to "get back to her own territory and if they refused I would use the atomic bomb on them while we have it and before they get it." He asserted that "If Russia had the atomic bomb there would be few Americans alive today." '[64] From the other side of the iron curtain Stalin bitterly attacked his former ally: 'Like Hitler . . . he also begins the work of unleashing a new war with a race theory, asserting that only English-speaking nations are full fledged nations, who are called upon to decide the fortunes of the entire world.'[65]

Four

THE COLD WAR INTENSIFIES

Stalin was inordinately suspicious of the West. Nevertheless there was some truth in his assessment of Anglo–American intentions. Truman's plan to force a Russian withdrawal from Eastern Europe had misfired. He still had enormous power at his disposal but it seemed to have little effect. Inexperienced in foreign affairs, he was acting in a piecemeal way, lacking a coherent policy. It is not surprising, therefore, that he found the Fulton speech 'admirable'. Reminding Americans that they stood 'at the pinnacle of world power', Churchill explained how best they could use that power. In effect, he urged them to check Communist expansion wherever it threatened. He was indeed suggesting that the Americans, together with the British Commonwealth, should 'decide the fortunes of the entire world' – in order, of course, to save it from the tyranny of Communism.

Such a global policy had been advocated by Kennan, Deputy Chief of Mission at the American Embassy in Moscow, in a paper he sent to the State Department in February 1946. In the words of Halle, who was then working there, it 'came at a moment when the Department, having been separated by circumstances from the wartime policy toward Russia, was floundering about, looking for new intellectual moorings . . . Now . . . it was offered a new and realistic conception . . . There was a universal feeling that "this was it", this was the appreciation of the situation that had been needed . . . We may not doubt that it made its effect on the President . . . From this notable document . . . dates the formulation of a new American and Western policy . . .'[1] Kennan reiterated Truman's belief that only a tough policy could be effective against the Soviet Union: 'Impervious to the logic of reason, it is highly sensitive to the logic of force.'[2] His analysis 'ended all hope of establishing conventional or "normal" . . . relations with this dark dictatorship, hag-ridden by the ghosts of the Russian past. . . .'[3] Whereas Truman had tried to force a contraction of Soviet influence, Kennan argued that the correct policy was to prevent its expansion. The Soviets should be resisted at all points. Such resistance, Kennan believed, would encourage the disruptive forces within the Soviet state. Here Kennan turns Marxism on its head, stating that not capitalism but Communism had within itself the seeds of its own decay. 'In the absence of a genuinely popular allegiance to the doctrines in which it clothes itself, its internal system is bound to be strained by "recent territorial expansions".'[4] Kennan implied that his policy, later described as containment, would in the long run force the whole Communist edifice to crumble.

As Ambrose points out, the habit of making such 'simplistic judgments about internal affairs in foreign countries was a phenomenon of American life. It was based, in part, on a world-view that other peoples yearned to be like Americans. This assumption was at the root of America's foreign policy. It denied historical and cultural diversity and led to the belief that when other nations . . . did not act like the United States it was because something had gone wrong, usually with the leadership. Americans found it impossible to believe that any people could actually want to be Communist.'[5]

We might note that, equally, they found it impossible to believe that the Russians could be other than expansionist. 'Whatever the merits,' says Fleming, 'of our Soviet world conquest belief, the reasons for it were seldom stated. Very early in the Cold War the idea became a slogan, an axiom, our main article of faith. It was simply asserted by virtually all of our leaders so many thousands of times, and carried into every mind by all the mass avenues of public information so often that only a few continued to question it.'[6] Thus it was simply assumed, for example, that Stalin was planning the invasion of Western Europe.

Many historians now reject that assumption. They stress the dreadful devastation suffered by the Soviet Union during the war,[7] which virtually ruled out any major offensive action when the war was over. 'In retrospect,' said Blackett in 1956, 'I find it impossible to believe that Western military experts can have thought in the least likely a Soviet land aggression against Western Europe after the War even if no atomic bombs had existed. All the military and material facts were against the possibility . . . If she had entertained the idea of conquering Western Europe by force, she would certainly have waited many years to recover from her war injuries and

A Greek view of the Civil War. The country, freed from the Nazis, is now a victim of royalist and communist extremists – the latter reaching for help from Bulgaria (on the back of Yugoslavia) while Albania watches through the fence. Britain and America are apparently plotting in their own interest.

to rebuild her country.'[8] Kennan, in 1965, made the same point. 'It was', he said, 'perfectly clear to anyone with even a rudimentary knowledge of the Russia of that day that the Soviet leaders had no intention of attempting to advance their cause by launching military attacks with their own armed forces across frontiers'.[9]

Hindsight is one of the occupational hazards of the historian. The judgment made by Kennan in 1965 should not tempt us to ignore the fears that underlay the policy he helped to shape some twenty years previously. Whether illusory or not, they were genuinely felt. As Halle has indicated: '. . . in the immediate aftermath of the War, Moscow appeared in the West to have extended its dominion to the shores of the Adriatic. In 1946 and 1947 it was easy to believe that Greece and then Italy would be the next to fall. And after that, perhaps, France.'[10]

At that time, Greece was seen as a critical area. In the words of Laqueur: 'During the first phase of the civil war in 1944–5 Stalin had loyally observed the agreement with Churchill according to which Greece was part of the British sphere of influence;[11] the Greek Communists received no help in their armed struggle against the government. The decision to renew the civil war was made in May 1946; it cannot have been taken without Soviet knowledge, and in all probability Soviet support. It was a deliberate decision, not a case of automatic escalation, and it was bound to lead to a major crisis.'[12]

There is no question that it did cause a major crisis, which resulted in the declaration of the Truman Doctrine. The point at issue is whether the crisis was provoked by Stalin. There is little evidence to support the almost unanimous Western view that he was to blame. On the other hand, it is easy to understand why the Greek Communists wanted to resume the civil war. Fleming has pointed out that '. . . Greece was the first of the liberated states to be openly and forcibly compelled to accept the political system of the occupying Great Power. It was Churchill who acted first and Stalin who followed his example, in Bulgaria and then in Rumania, though with less bloodshed.'[13] In the winter of 1944–5 the British bloodily suppressed left-wing forces in Greece, including Communists, in an attempt to safeguard their interests in the area.[14] To quote Fleming again: 'Greece was in effect a British colony. Its public utilities, shipping and insurance were dominated by the British, who held a third of the Greek national debt and controlled one of its main banks. Greece was a part of Britain's imperial heritage . . .'[15]

Tsaldaris, Churchill's Prime Minister, silenced opposition to the discredited monarchy, which had returned in the wake of the British forces. His government ignored the country's acute social and economic problems. An American eye-witness commented: 'There are few modern parallels for government as bad as this.'[16] In the circumstances it was certain that the Greek Communists and their supporters would take advantage of the growing weakness of the British to try to overthrow a government which was regarded even by neutral observers as outstandingly reactionary.

Characteristically, Stalin showed little enthusiasm for their cause. O'Ballance says that he '. . . vaguely promised to help, but no supplies or arms ever arrived from the Soviet Union'.[17] According to Djilas: 'The Soviet Government took no direct action over the uprising in Greece. . . .'[18] Stalin did ask Yugoslavia and Albania to give clandestine support to the insurgents. That was the least he could do and the most he would do. In the very month when a referendum officially restored King George to the Greek throne, Stalin showed his readiness to co-operate with the King's Western protectors. 'I do not doubt', he said, 'that the possibilities of peaceful co-operation [with the Western democracies], far from decreasing may even grow. Communism in one country is perfectly possible, especially in a country like the Soviet Union.'[19] The London *Times* described his statement as 'a timely and much needed recall to sanity and moderation in international relations'.[20] His conciliatory mood was reinforced in December 1946 by agreement on the treaties with Germany's satellites. This 'was accompanied by a real relaxation of tension on Russia's side. The Soviets felt assured that their influence would be predominant in Eastern Europe. Their primary war aim had been achieved.'[21]

McNeill has neatly summarized the position: 'In general it seems reasonable to suppose that Stalin had not explicitly and definitely given up the idea of world revolution any more than he had definitely and explicitly abandoned hope of continued co-operation with Britain and America. Yet, as in the past, he put the security of the Soviet Union before all else.'[22]

While events in Europe encouraged Soviet moderation, elections in the USA impelled Truman to persist with his hard line. In November 1946 the Republican Party gained control of Congress for the first time since 1928. 'Most political analysts shared the view of columnist Marquis Childs that "the cry of communism which was raised by Republicans from one side of the country to the other" played a large part in [their] victory.'[23] Desperate to regain power, the Republicans unfairly but successfully accused the Democrats of being 'soft on Communists'.[24] Truman responded swiftly. On 25 November he set up a Temporary Commission on Employee Loyalty to advise him on combating 'subversion' within the civil service. A few months later he ordered 2,500,000 government employees to undergo a new security check. 'The President's motivation was scarcely veiled. "Well, that should take the Communist smear off the Democratic party!" he said.'[25] In fact it did not – the dark days of McCarthyism lay in the future; the era of the loyalty oath had only begun. Truman's reaction to the Republican stratagem did ensure that in the United States 'nobody could be elected unless he publicly detested the Russians and nothing could be done unless it would injure or displease the Russians.'[26]

In effect, the Republicans had advanced a conspiracy theory – that Americans' troubles stemmed from Communists in their midst. Truman, instead of attacking it, pandered to it. In doing so, he helped to propagate another conspiracy theory, which he himself seemed to accept, that every international problem had its origin in the Kremlin. Thus it followed that the civil war in Greece was quite simply a Soviet plot to expand in the Eastern Mediterranean. Unlike some other observers of the Greek conflict, the American leaders were convinced that Stalin had been the prime mover.[27]

They had prepared accordingly. In September 1946 programmes for military aid to Greece had been drawn up. An economic mission had been sent in January of the following year and in February 1947 the tempo of the contingency planning increased. The United States was prepared to move into Greece whenever the British pulled out.[28]

The Second World War had drained the British economy. 'At the end of the war Britain was transformed from being a lender to the world to the amount of £4,000 million, to being a debtor to the amount of £3,000 million!'[29] Since 1945 the Labour government had been beset by economic crises. A disastrously severe winter in 1946–7, which paralysed British industry for weeks, forced the British to realize how vulnerable they were and compelled them to reduce their commitments overseas. At the end of February they warned the Americans that they could no longer afford to maintain troops in Greece. The expected American reaction was expressed succinctly by Acheson, then Under-Secretary of State: 'The British are getting out of Turkey and Greece and if we don't go in the Russians will.'[30] That was the genesis of the Truman Doctrine.

The Doctrine was stated in a speech Truman delivered, on 12 March 1947, to both Houses of Congress.[31] Although it was prompted by the Greek crisis, he clearly intended it to have a wider relevance. In his memoirs he says: 'I wanted no hedging in this speech. This was America's answer to the surge of expansion of Communist tyranny. It had to be clear and free of hesitation or double talk.'[32] Specifically, he asked Congress to approve a first outlay of $400 million for assistance to Greece and Turkey. He also sought its approval for the use of American civilian and military personnel to help the reconstruction of both countries and to supervise the handling of the aid provided. Earlier in the speech he explained that America should give help to any country that was threatened by Communism. He made it clear that he thought the only choice was between 'democracy' and 'totalitarianism'.

'At the present moment in world history,' he said, 'nearly every nation must choose between alternative ways of life. The choice is too often not a free one. One way of life is based upon the will of the majority, and is distinguished by free institutions, representative government, free elections, guarantees of individual liberty, freedom of speech and religion, and freedom from political oppression. The second way of life is based upon the will of a minority, forcibly imposed upon the majority. It relies upon terror and oppression, a controlled press and radio, fixed elections and the suppression of personal freedoms'. The essence of the doctrine was in the next statement: 'I believe that it must be the policy of the United States to support free peoples who are resisting attempted subjugation by armed minorities or by outside pressures.'[33]

As Ambrose says: 'The statement was all-encompassing. In a single sentence, Truman had defined American foreign policy for the next twenty years.'[34] There can be no argument on that point. Whether the policy was a good one, and what prompted it, are more contentious issues. The received view among Western historians is that Truman's speech simply recognized that it was not possible to deal reasonably with the Russians. Describing the period 1946–7, Laqueur notes: 'The Soviet stand became more and more adamant, despite constant, often pathetic Western attempts to reach compromises and to allay Soviet suspicions.'[35] The Greek crisis, it is argued, abruptly forced the democracies to see the light. 'It is essential,' says Donnelly, 'to grasp the sudden transformation that took place in Washington in early 1947.'[36] Halle also stresses the immediacy of the decision: 'This was once more the eleventh hour – as in 1917, as in 1941. If the United States did not intervene now, all would be lost.'[37] Truman acted and all was saved. 'As has been the case more than once in our time, the cohorts of freedom overcame their normal demoralization and disarray at the eleventh hour.'[38] According to these opinions, Truman intervened in the nick of time to underpin the integrity of Greece and Turkey and to promote the cause of freedom throughout the world.

That interpretation has been questioned at several points. First, that Truman did not undergo a sudden conversion under extreme Soviet pressure. Alperovitz remarks: 'Truman's own argument that a stable Europe was vital to world peace and to American security reveals the error of the common opinion that America had little active interest in European affairs until the 1947 Truman Doctrine and Marshall Plan. The President's mid-1945 declaration to his staff was an accurate statement of American policy: "We were committed to the rehabilitation of Europe, and there was to be no abandonment this time." '³⁹ Secondly, the Doctrine was formulated at a time when the Russians seemed to favour conciliation rather than confrontation. Howard Smith records that at the Moscow Conference of Foreign Ministers, which opened just before Truman made his speech: 'Molotov proved uncommonly conciliatory in the opening discussion . . . The Russians undoubtedly assumed that all was well and that things would go according to prescription . . . two years of haggling and pressuring until deadlock was reached, then settlement on that basis.' However: 'Right on top of the conference . . . burst the bombshell of the Truman Doctrine . . . it sounded like an ultimatum to the rest of Europe to be with us or to be counted against us. That wiped the smiles off the Russians' faces.'⁴⁰

Apart from its timing, the Doctrine's intentions are also open to question. Did the 'obligation to combat totalitarian régimes extend to Spain, Portugal and Argentina ? The country had a right to know if the President was talking "about all totalitarian régimes imposed by the will of the minority or only about a certain variety of totalitarian régimes imposed by a certain kind of minority".'⁴¹ Walter Lippmann assumed, correctly, that Truman was prepared to support any régime so long as it was anti-Communist, and argued that: 'The basic fallacy of the Truman Doctrine lay in its assumption that the spread of communism could be checked by subsidizing the reactionary forces of the world.'⁴² The open-ended nature of Truman's pledge of assistance also disturbed a British diplomat who commented that 'the policy of aid to Greece was made to seem hardly less than a declaration of war on the Soviet Union'.⁴³

Such criticisms did not prevent Truman from getting what he wanted. 'For the first time in its history, the United States had chosen to intervene in a period of general peace in the affairs of peoples outside North and South America.'⁴⁴ Of course Truman's administration had been intervening in the affairs of Europe and Asia since 1945. The policy of containment had been elaborated long before his speech to Congress. But it was virtually unknown to the public who, even early in 1947, were not keen to embark on an anti-Communist crusade. 'To obtain the economic and military resources to carry out an active foreign policy, Truman had to convince the bulk of the people of the reality and magnitude of the Soviet threat.'⁴⁵ He had, in Vandenberg's phrase, to 'scare hell out of the American people.'[46] That helps to explain why, instead of asking them to 'support a rather shabby king', he described the Greek situation 'in universal terms, good versus evil . . .'[47] He was brilliantly successful. Anti-Communism became the hallmark of Americanism. The premises of his doctrine were accepted and there was, for a long time, to be no turning back.

Soviet reaction was expressed in the official newspaper *Izvestia*: 'Dilations to the effect that the USA is called upon to "save" Greece and Turkey from expansion on the part of so-called "totalitarian" States are not new. Hitler also referred to the Bolsheviks when he wanted to open the road to conquests for himself. Now they try to take Greece and Turkey under their control and by raising a clamour about "totalitarian States", attempt to disguise their plans for expansion. This seems the more attractive in that, while elbowing themselves in, the USA is pushing non-totalitarian Great Britain out of yet another State or two . . . We witness a fresh intrusion of the USA into the affairs of other States.'[48]

Ironically, though predictably, the Truman Doctrine, which was aimed at containing Russian imperialism, provoked Soviet fears of American imperialism. *Izvestia*'s analysis of US intentions was, in Russian eyes, corroborated by the next great American initiative, the Marshall Plan. In the words of Fleming : 'If the Marshall invitation had been issued before the Truman Doctrine, or rather in lieu of it, the Cold War might have been averted. Coming after the recent promulgation of the Truman Doctrine the Soviets were bound to scrutinize it with extra suspicion, to see if it might be a means of implementing the Doctrine.'[49] Like Truman, the Russians regarded both policies as part of the same grand design – two halves of the same walnut, in his phrase. Thus Malenkov's attack on the plan echoed *Izvestia*'s critique of the doctrine: 'The ruling clique of American imperialists . . . has taken the path of outright expansionism . . . The clearest and most specific expression of the policy . . . is provided by the Truman–Marshall plans . . . plans for a new war against the Soviet Union and the new democracies are being hatched . . .'[50]

In his speech, on 5 June 1947, proposing the plan to bear his name, Marshall had declared: 'Our policy is directed not against any country or doctrine but against hunger, poverty, desperation and chaos.'[51] On 1 July he emphatically rejected the Soviet allegations of expansionism: 'There could be no more fantastic misrepresenta-

Two architects of the Western Alliance, US Secretary of State, George Marshall and British Foreign Secretary, Ernest Bevin.

tion, no more malicious distortion of the truth, than the frequent propaganda assertions . . . that the USA has imperialist aims or that American aid has been offered in order to fasten on the recipients some form of political and economic domination.'[52]

What was the truth behind the rhetoric? Churchill was convinced that the plan was 'the most unselfish act in history'. The United States was offering to finance, from its ample resources, the reconstruction of the war-racked continent of Europe. Truman, who knew rather more about it, had a somewhat different view. His objective was economic reconstruction with a political purpose – to 'save Europe from economic disaster and [lift] from it the shadow of enslavement by Russian Communism'.[53] In practice, aid went only to one part of Europe. 'I think', says Truman, 'the world now realizes that without the Marshall Plan it would have been difficult for Western Europe to remain free from the tyranny of Communism'.[54]

It seems clear that there was no intention of giving help to the Communist part of Europe, or to the Soviet Union. Kennan, who had been charged with producing a plan for the aid, made it very difficult for the Russians to accept American help. He required them to make available their economic records for scrutiny and, in effect, to open the markets of Eastern Europe to American business men. If the Soviets had agreed to his terms they would have weakened their hold over an area vital to their own security. It seems likely that the State Department was opposed in fact to Soviet participation in the Marshall Plan: that they made conditions they knew would be unacceptable but which put the onus of refusal on the Russians.[55]

This helps to explain why the American planners bypassed the United Nations Economic Commission for Europe. They wanted to ensure that no aid went to the Soviets and thus required complete control over its distribution.[56]

There is little doubt that the plan, despite Marshall's demurrer, was anti-Soviet, a 'move to consolidate Western Europe as a counter-weight to the concentration of Russian power in the East . . .'[57] It was also, according to some commentators, a move to stimulate the US economy and to consolidate American influence in Western Europe. While the plan was being discussed in Congress, the *United States News* declared: 'If world buying power is exhausted, world markets for US goods would disappear. The real idea behind the program, thus, is that the United States, to prevent a depression at home must put up the dollars that it will take to prevent a collapse abroad. The real argument for the support of the Marshall Plan is the bolstering of the American system for future years.'[58]

Greene alleges that: 'Marshall Plan aid, essentially intended to keep the post-war economies of the West Europe countries within the capitalist world, was also intended to dominate their economy. Every transaction was arranged to provide not only immediate profits . . . for specific US banks, finance corporations, investment trusts and industries, but to make the European nations dependent on the United States.'[59] In *The Tragedy of American Diplomacy* Williams comments that 'in expanding its own economic system throughout much of the world, America has made it very difficult for other nations to retain any economic independence'.[60] He goes on to say: 'Most Americans agreed with Secretary of State James Byrnes, who remarked in July 1945, that the problem was "not to make the world safe for democracy, but to make the world safe for the United States". It was simply assumed that the two things were the same.'[61]

In 1947, beset with economic problems and with few resources to solve them, Western European leaders were not disposed to question American motives. They accepted the offer of aid with alacrity. Bevin and Bidault drew up a plan based on the principle of integrating national economies. Molotov, to the relief of the Western leaders, rejected it.[62] The manner and nature of his rejection seemed to justify all the West's fears of Soviet intentions. Describing the event in 1949 Smith wrote: 'He left Paris in a huff and did not allow the Russian satellite nations to accept invitations to a . . . conference to lay . . . plans for accepting the Marshall offer. Three months later, Russia organized the *Cominform* and frankly declared war on the Marshall Plan . . . the West . . . could come to no other conclusion than that Russia was opposed to the reconstruction of Europe and desired a state of disruption in order to win Europe for Communism.'[63]

Legend:
- ——— Pre-war frontiers
- •••••• The Iron Curtain
- Annexed by Russia
- Russian Occupation Zones
  - ① Germany
  - ② Austria
- Russian dominated communist regimes imposed by Stalin

FINLAND

ESTONIA

LATVIA

LITH.

Moscow

P O L A N D

Berlin

Br.

①

CZECHOSLOVAKIA

Fr.

U.S.

U.S. ②

Fr.

Br.

HUNGARY

RUMANIA

I T A L Y

Y U G O S L A V I A

BULGARIA

ALBANIA

GREECE

TURKEY

Mediterranean   Sea

Five

THE SOVIETS IN EASTERN EUROPE

It was, in fact, highly unlikely that the Russians would communize Western Europe. The odds against a military takeover were, as we have seen, very high. As late as 1949 even Dulles discounted that possibility. 'So far as it is humanly possible to judge,' he said, 'the Soviet Government, under conditions now prevailing, does not contemplate the use of war as an instrument of its national policy. I do not know any responsible official, military or civilian, in this Government or any Government who believes that the Soviet Government now plans conquest by open military aggression.'[1] There was no other way for the Soviets to enlarge their sphere of influence. Virtually all the economic weapons were in the hands of the Americans. Indeed, as Marshall Aid began to flow, the Russians, far from threatening the West, felt themselves threatened by the West. Their objective was not expansion but consolidation of their existing control over Eastern Europe.

Whether Stalin, from the first, intended to create a Soviet empire in Eastern Europe is arguable. Pethybridge argues against that view: 'Stalin's geographical manipulations in Poland showed that at the beginning he had no precise plans for forcing a Communist government on that country. He annoyed the Poles by refusing to make any concessions about their eastern frontier. Yet if Poland as well as Russia were to be part of a new Communist commonwealth, what need was there for Stalin to be so adamant? Soviet relations with Communist parties in the Axis countries were also strained because of the crippling reparations that Stalin demanded from Hungary, Rumania and Bulgaria. There would have been little reason to ransack and antagonize Eastern Europe if Stalin had already envisaged the pattern of Soviet economic control that evolved in the area after the war.'[2]

However, as Pethybridge points out, Stalin changed his mind: '. . . before long he was to extend Socialism in One Country to Socialism in One Zone on a systematic basis. Stalin was to discover that the only way he could ensure undisputed Soviet influence in Eastern Europe was to apply controlled revolution from above.'[3] Significantly, the controls were imposed after the announcement of the Truman Doctrine and the Marshall Plan. Obvious threats to Soviet influence, they ensured the satellization of the countries of Eastern Europe. The coalition governments were destroyed and Communist party dictatorship imposed. Non-Communist politicians were charged with complicity in plots, some genuine, most of them manufactured, against the state. The resignation or dismissal of non-Communists allowed the Communists to assume complete control. Thus, in May 1947, Ferenc Nagy, while on holiday in Switzerland, gave up the premiership of Hungary.[4] In resigning by telephone he avoided arrest or death. Petkov, an opposition leader in Bulgaria, was not so fortunate. Arrested in June 1947, he was hanged in September.[5] In December Bulgaria was proclaimed a People's Republic.[6] Mikolajczyk, leader of the Peasant Party in Poland, avoided a similar fate by fleeing to the West in October 1947.[7] Maniu, the 74-year-old head of the Rumanian Peasant Party, was sentenced to life imprisonment in November and in December Rumania too became a People's Republic.[8]

Stalin had been merciless in imposing his control over the Soviet Union. His henchmen in Eastern Europe were as unscrupulous, almost, as their master. Western observers stressed the contrast between the democratic and the Communist way. Halle describes how, in the winter of 1947–8, they began to understand the 'nature of the police administration that had descended on Eastern Europe, that had made of it virtually a complex of concentration camps...'[9]

In 1949, Spaak was to remark that 'half Europe, composed of countries close to us by virtue of their civilization and history, had fallen into slavery'.[10]

Such reactions were natural but somewhat exaggerated and misleading. Eastern Europe, *pace* Spaak, was very different from Western Europe. Except in Czechoslovakia and Finland there was, for example, no tradition of democracy. 'The old masters of Eastern Europe,' says Smith, 'maintained control over their inevitably . . . discontented peoples by three means. First by the sheer force of . . . ruthless rural gendarmeries and over-sized corrupt bureaucracies. Second, by illiteracy: in wide sections of the area it was higher than in Spain and Portugal. Third, by canalizing discontent into anti-semitism in Poland and Hungary, into regional antagonisms as in Yugoslavia, and into chauvinism everywhere . . . The potentially democratic forces which might have challenged this sick old order were too weak or divided to do so.'[11] Smith doubts whether the events of the war had done much to strengthen such forces: 'It is very easy to criticize the course of the Communists in Rumania, but it is very hard to think of any constructive alternatives. Free elections would have been an invitation to Fascism . . .'[12] Much the same could be said for other iron curtain countries, with the exception of Czechoslovakia. According to Smith: 'The Iron Curtain . . . has existed as long as European civilization. As long as that have tyrants and ruling cliques been oppressing . . . their opponents behind it . . . The only new thing . . . is the West's admirable but conspicuously sudden concern for its victims.'[13]

Another new feature was Western concern for the national integrity of the iron curtain countries. In pursuit of a Soviet empire Stalin, it was said, reduced them to colonial status. There is much truth in this: there is also some hypocrisy. Singleton has pointed out that 'the peoples of Eastern Europe have seldom been allowed to express their aspirations freely, without outside interference. In recent times this has meant that the development of the resources of the area has been undertaken less for the benefit of the inhabitants than as a means of furthering the interests of the industrially more developed nations of Western Europe. Apart from a few areas in Poland, Hungary, Bohemia and Slovenia, manufacturing industry on a large scale has only begun since the end of the Second World War. Formerly the role of Eastern Europe in the economy of the whole continent was that of a supplier of food and raw materials to its more affluent Western neighbours.'[14] As Smith comments: 'The area has . . . been largely an economic colony of the West, with France, Britain, Germany and America owning most of its worthwhile assets.'[15]

It is worth noting, moreover, that during the Second World War the ruling classes in Eastern Europe, who had acquiesced in the economic domination of the Western powers, supported one of those powers, Germany, when it tried to destroy the Soviet Union. Bulgaria, Hungary and Rumania had been Nazi satellites. Rumania indeed 'was Germany's outstanding ally, supplying more combat troops and conquering more territory for the Axis than did

Italy. Rumanian armies fought deep in the Soviet Caucasus and . . . annexed a large slice of the Soviet Ukraine . . . the area was thoroughly plundered . . . and mass executions were carried out on the German model.'[16]

Such facts do not excuse the brutal terrorism of Stalin's satraps, the midnight arrests, the rigged trials, the concentration camps and the execution squads. The Rakosi régime that Stalin foisted on Hungary was as merciless as the Batista clique that the Americans tolerated in Cuba.* Even so, it is unhelpful to interpret events in Eastern Europe, as Seton-Watson does, simply in terms of the Communists' 'lust for power'.[17] To describe land reform solely as 'an instrument of Communist power' is to concentrate unduly on the political issues.[18] It undervalues the social and economic consequences of a policy that was only in part politically motivated. Describing the Communist régimes in the Balkan region, Stavrianos points out that the 'political revolution was accompanied by – indeed it made possible – a corresponding economic upheaval.'[19] He claims that: 'The institutions and traditions of a millenium have been revolutionized before our eyes during the brief period since the Balkan Peninsula was engulfed in World War II.'[20]

Nettl has described the means of fastening Soviet control on Eastern Europe as 'a dominant Party, industrializing from above, eliminating its opponents one by one, and creating the basis of a socialist society in a hurry'.[21] The attempt to create a socialist society in such a backward area involved fundamental changes. Under Stalin it led to the setting up of concentration camps. But to dismiss Eastern Europe as 'virtually a complex of concentration camps' was also to ignore the social and economic revolution that accompanied the police terror. That was precisely the error made by many Western leaders from 1947 onwards. It was a serious underestimation of the challenge posed by the Communists.

In Smith's estimation: '. . . the potentialities for social expansion in Eastern Europe awaited only a constructive leadership. The job did not call specifically for the Communists.'[22] However, instead of recognizing that there was a need for drastic change, Western politicians saw only the ugly concomitants of a social revolution effected in the Stalinist manner. This led some of them to further

* On US support for Batista, and on the brutality of his régime see R. Scheer and M. Zeitlin, *Cuba: An American Tragedy*, pp. 54–7, Penguin, 1964; also H. Thomas, *Cuba or The Pursuit of Freedom*, pp. 789–90 and p. 1073, Eyre & Spottiswoode, 1971.

errors of judgment. First, they were persuaded that Eastern Europe might be ripe for 'liberation'. Secondly, they came to believe that no demands for basic changes were genuine; they were simply stratagems of Communists or fellow-travellers to further the cause of world-wide Communism. Thus, in Greece, Truman supported régimes that were as oppressive as the governments of their Communist neighbours but which were acceptable because they were strongly anti-Communist. Their resistance to demands for fundamental reforms was taken as proof of their political reliability. In waging his anti-Communist crusade, Truman, as we have already noted, 'allied himself with reaction around the globe'. .

America's tough anti-Soviet policy encouraged the hard-liners in the Kremlin. Deutscher observes: '. . . the bogy the West had invoked to justify the Truman Doctrine – the Red Hordes threatening Europe – assumed some reality . . .'[23] In September 1947 the Communist Information Bureau, the Cominform, was established.[24] It was to 'co-ordinate the activities of the Communist parties' of the Soviet Union and its satellites. Also included in it were the French and Italian parties. Zhdanov, one of the Soviet delegates to the founding conference, commented: 'A new alignment of political forces has arisen. The more the war recedes into the past, the more distinct become two major trends in post-war international policy, corresponding to the division of the political forces operating on the international arena into two major camps; the imperialist and anti-democratic camp, on the one hand and the anti-imperialist and democratic camp, on the other. The principal driving force of the imperialist camp is the USA . . . The cardinal purpose of the imperialist camp is to strengthen imperialism, to hatch a new imperialist war, to combat Socialism and democracy . . .'[25] In the opinion of the *New York Times*, the Soviet move was 'a clear declaration of political war.'[26] The West saw the Cominform as an instrument for the farther extension of Soviet influence in Europe and the complete subordination of all Communist parties to the interests of the Soviet Union. As we have seen, events in Bulgaria, Hungary, Poland and Rumania confirmed that impression. It was, however, Czechoslovakia that provided the most blatant example of the new Soviet policy in action.

In 1946 the Communists in Czechoslovakia had gained 38 percent of the vote in a genuinely free election.[27] Under the Communist premier, Gottwald, a coalition government carried out a programme of land reform and nationalization of major industries which had mass support. However, the country was still suffering from the effects of the war and by early 1948 the difficulties of the government were reducing its popularity. At the forthcoming election it seemed likely that the Communists would lose many votes. The economic troubles might have been relieved by Marshall Aid but, under Soviet pressure, the government had refused it. The Russians evidently feared that events in France and Italy, where Communists had been ousted from coalitions, might be repeated in Czechoslovakia. If the Communist vote fell, the other parties might be able to form a government that would, after all, join the Marshall Plan. Even at the end of 1947 some three-quarters of Czech foreign trade was carried on with the West.[28] The twin dangers of electoral defeat and Western penetration were avoided by a Communist seizure of power.

Smith, an eye-witness of the event, noted: 'For pure craftsman-ship this *coup d'etat* was stunning.'[29] With the minimum of fuss and no bloodshed, 'the Czech Communist Party succeeded in taking over the country with only the sympathetic surveillance and advice of the Soviet Embassy.'[30] There was virtually no opposition. Smith records: 'When the Nazis marched into the country, the Czechs wept as they lined the streets, and cursed their oppressors openly. While walking the streets from dawn till dusk for all five days of the crisis, I saw no single person weeping, nor, in fact, any expression of anger. The walls remained clean of chalked slogans for or against the *coup*.'[31] We cannot here examine in depth the reasons for such acquiescence. One writer has emphasized 'the traumatic experience of Munich'. He suggests that: 'To many non-Communist Czechs – who may since have changed their minds – affinity with the Soviet Union was simply preferable to affinity with the West. The bitter fruit of pre-war anti-Soviet policies was being reaped.'[32]

The *coup* made no fundamental change in the balance of power between Russia and America: 'it was . . . a closing operation to complete the organization of the socialist bloc rather than the beginning of a new offensive against capitalist states.'[33] Even so, it had a great effect on those states. In the words of Horowitz: '. . . with no counter-balancing European power in sight, in the wake of massive strikes led by native Communist parties in France and Italy, the Soviets subverted the democratically elected pro-

Prime Minister Gottwald announces the formation of the new Communist government to crowds in Wenceslaus Square, Prague.

Soviet Government of the one central European state which had become the symbol of the whole disastrous slide into the Second World War . . . Thus . . . the *coup* in Czechoslovakia strengthened the hand of every die-hard anti-Bolshevik and extreme nationalist in the Western camp. In the wake of this event, the liberal left entered into an alliance with the reactionary right . . . Russian "aggression", though in areas behind the Iron Curtain, served to underwrite every catastrophic step taken in the West towards massive re-armament . . .'[34] Horowitz goes on to argue that, while the Czech affair encouraged the advocates of re-armament, another event indicated that the West was, in fact, already adequately equipped to deter Soviet aggression. He refers to the split between Yugoslavia and the Soviet Union.

In June 1948 Yugoslavia was expelled from the Cominform, essentially because Tito refused to be a Russian puppet.[35] Unlike Stalin's creatures in other iron-curtain countries he had made his own revolution. His partisans, not the Red Army, had created a socialist Yugoslavia. He had the support of the mass of his people and had his own plans for his own country.

Tito's independent attitude brought a clash with Stalin as early as 1945. At that time Stalin suggested that, after the war, King Peter should be restored in Yugoslavia.[36] Outraged, Tito rejected the suggestion. It was remarkable that Stalin ever made it: it indicates, what we have seen elsewhere, how little Stalin was concerned with promoting or supporting revolutions, unless he had complete control over them. Despite him, the revolution did take place and Tito remained as leader of Yugoslavia when the war was over. He remained loyal, but not subservient, to the Soviet Union. As the Cold War developed his relations with the West were as hostile as Stalin

Marshal Tito with the headquarters staff of his National Liberation Army in 1944.

might have wished. Indeed Tito showed less regard for Western sensibilities than did Stalin. When American planes persisted in flying over Yugoslavia he had several of them shot down. While Stalin virtually ignored the Greek Communists, Tito gave them considerable support and allowed their troops to take refuge in Yugoslavia when they were hard pressed. In their foreign policy the Yugoslavs were steadfast defenders of the interests of the Communist bloc. The charge that was levelled at Tito by Stalin, that he was an imperialist agent, was utterly absurd.[37] It was made not because of his non-existent links with the West but because of his unharmonious relations with the Soviet Union. On several issues he disagreed with the Russians and showed no signs of repenting. He refused to be a Soviet lackey and was therefore accused of being a traitor to the cause of Communism.

Soviet policy was to undermine Tito's position in his own country. Unscrupulous efforts were made to split the Yugoslav Communist Party, to create conflict among its leaders and to encourage a Stalinist *coup*. Stalin allegedly believed that he would shake his little finger and there would be no more Tito.[38] The Russians mobilized support among their satellites in Eastern Europe: the heretic was vilified by the faithful but refused to recant. Ordinary party members and the people of Yugoslavia must have been bewildered by the whole affair. They had been told that Soviet Russia was the great ally and that Comrade Stalin was the infallible leader of World Communism. They knew little of the conflicts that preceded the split and must have been shocked by its suddenness; the quarrel with Russia caused a conflict of loyalties. However, given the history of the country, it was likely that national sentiment, particularly strong after the wartime experience, would be more powerful than loyalty to Stalin. As a former expert on the national question, Stalin might have anticipated that outcome. In fact he underestimated the powerful appeal of Tito and the personal loyalty of the Yugoslav leaders who had been his comrades during the war.[39]

Once the attempt at subversion had failed Stalin might have been expected to play his trump card – the Red Army, which the West feared so much. Surely such a formidable force could subdue the Yugoslavs. In fact no military action was taken. Horowitz comments that 'the failure of the Red Army or of any of the satellite armies to invade the renegade state . . . could mean only one of two things. Either the Soviets were not willing to invade a country presenting a strong national front – or *already existing American military power* was sufficient to deter Stalin from any armed aggression in Europe. Thus *before* Nato, *before* Western and West German re-armament, *before* the spiralling and debilitating arms race had seized hold of Europe, Communist power was adequately and effectively "contained" by the greater and more vastly extended power of the US.'[40]

Truman, in 1948, thought otherwise and 'with invaluable assistance from Soviet actions' was able to persuade the United States to join NATO and to re-arm on a vast scale. The event that seemed to justify his policy was the Berlin Blockade. Having expelled Tito from the Cominform, Stalin tried to force the Western powers to withdraw from their sectors of West Berlin. To understand why he created the crisis which proved so convenient for Truman we must backtrack to examine what had happened in Germany.

Six

THE GERMAN PROBLEM

In April 1945 Stalin anticipated what would happen in Germany after the defeat of the Nazis. 'This war,' he said, 'is not as in the past; whoever occupies a territory also imposes on it his own social system. Everyone imposes his own system as far as his army has power to do so. It cannot be otherwise.'[1] The Red Army had played the major role in the destruction of the Wehrmacht and Stalin hoped that its presence in the centre of Europe would enable him to control the whole of Germany. For a time the Soviets favoured a united Germany, united of course on their own terms. His own assumption, however, that occupying powers would impose their own system, suggested that in fact Germany would be divided. The Americans, the British and the French, who occupied Western Germany, would prevent it falling into the Russian orbit.

Stalin's main objective was not, in any case, the unification of Germany but the security of the Soviet Union. Twenty million Russians died in the course of the Second World War. The first priority for the Soviets was, not surprisingly, to neutralize the German menace. Hence Stalin's policy of destroying Germany's economic power. He had no illusions, however, about the limitations of that policy. Dismissing suggestions that the Germans would take fifty years to reconstruct their economy, he commented: 'No, they will recover, and very quickly. It is a highly developed industrial country with an extremely skilled and numerous working class and technical intelligentsia. Give them twelve to fifteen years and they'll be on their feet again.'[2] Thus it was imperative, for Soviet security, to control the part of Germany that was already occupied by the Red Army. As the Cold War developed, the Western powers, for security motives of their own, made sure that their part of Germany was reliably anti-Soviet. Early in 1948 Stalin summed up the situation: 'The West will make Western Germany their own, and we shall turn Eastern Germany into our own state.'[3] Very soon after the end of the World War the powers which had united to defeat Germany were, like Germany itself, divided. For the West, Communism replaced Nazism as the main enemy. The Soviets still feared German militarism but principally as a potential accomplice of American imperialism. A brief examination of post-war developments in Germany may help to illustrate these new dispositions.

In 1945 Germany was divided into four zones of occupation which were controlled by Allied Military Governments. The three major powers had agreed that one zone should be given to France. Like the Russians, the French had been occupied by the Nazis and had indeed been invaded by the Germans three times since 1870. At first, French policy towards Germany was similar to the Soviet line, in that they both were determined to make Germans pay to the full for the devastation they had caused. The zones occupied by France and the Soviet Union were economically more viable than the other two zones. In the Soviet zone the economy was 'well balanced, having enough agriculture to feed itself . . .'[4] The French zone contained only 6,400,000 inhabitants and included the important Saar region. By contrast, the British zone contained 22,000,000 people and produced only 40 per cent of its own food. Although the US zone was slightly smaller than the British in terms of population and produced more of its own food, it was still not self-sufficient.[5]

The result was that the British and the Americans had to import food, at their own expense, into their zones. At the same time, the other two occupying powers took advantage of surpluses in their zones to exact the maximum reparations payments. The French 'began . . . the practice . . . of taking reparations not only of German capital machinery, but from current production.'[6] The Soviets 'removed whole plants to Russia' and 'milked their zone very nearly dry.'[7] Northedge comments that '. . . British subsidies to West Germany were compared to the hard-earned food supplied by a farmer to his cow while somebody else milked it at the other end.'[8]

Naturally the British, suffering austerity themselves, were aggrieved. However, as Smith remarks: 'It was asking the impossible to demand that Russia abandon her fortunate position in Germany in order to . . . stop the flow of reparations to Russia and perhaps cripple herself in order to raise the level of Germans who were responsible for Russia's predicament.'[9] In any case, the

USA, in denying post-war credits on acceptable terms, had virtually forced the Russians to rely on reparations. Ambrose records that '. . . in 1945 the Soviets asked for a one billion dollar loan. The United States government lost the request. When it was finally found, months later, the State Department offered to discuss the loan if the Soviets would pledge "non discrimination in international commerce", allowing American investment and goods into the Russian sphere of influence. Stalin rejected the offer . . . The Russians would rebuild through forced savings at home, at the expense of their own citizens, and by taking whatever they could from the European areas they occupied.'[10]

In March 1946 Clay, the military governor of the US zone, withheld shipments of Soviet reparations, to which they were entitled under the Potsdam agreements. This move was in retaliation for the Soviet breach of the agreements in refusing to supply foodstuffs from their zone and in taking reparations from current production. The fact was that the agreements were interpreted by each side to suit its own plans. Differences in economic policy reflected growing political disharmony (Clay's decision, for instance, coincided with Churchill's Fulton speech).

Schlesinger, commenting on the causes of Soviet discontent, says: 'The Russian hope for major Western assistance in post-war reconstruction foundered on three events which the Kremlin could well have interpreted respectively as deliberate sabotage (the loan request), blackmail (lend-lease cancellation) and pro-Germanism (reparations).'[11] A speech by Byrnes, on 6 September 1946, urging the need for German recovery, was indeed seen as 'the official inauguration of a pro-German American policy.'[12] The Russians were not alone in finding that policy unacceptable. In France, for example, the press was almost unanimous in declaring that 'the USA had forgotten the sufferings to which France and other former occupied territories had been subjected . . . and was apparently more concerned with helping Germany to become strong again.'[13]

The Americans, for their part, objected to pouring dollars into Germany while the Soviets, whom they increasingly distrusted, were taking all that they could from their zone. By making West Germany self-sufficient they could relieve themselves of a financial burden and acquire a useful ally in the political struggle. Unlike the Soviets, the Americans did not fear a revival of German

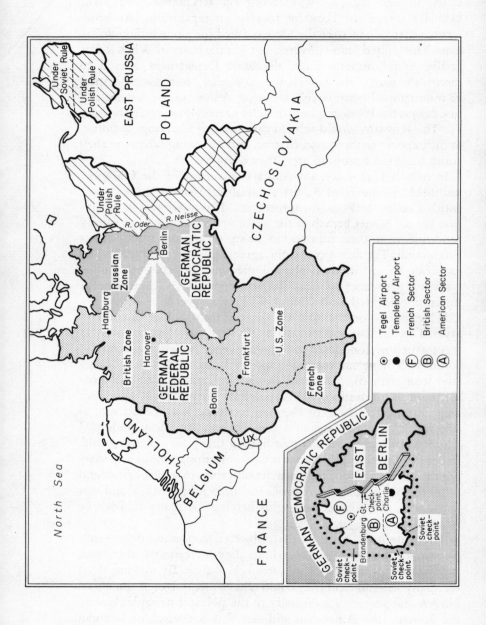

militarism. As Truman had said to de Gaulle in 1945: 'The German menace should not be exaggerated – the United States possessed a new weapon, the atomic bomb, which would defeat any aggressor.'[14] In 1946 the US, exaggerating the new Soviet menace, was indeed ready to seek German support. Clay's opinion was clear. Believing that the Germans were probably the only continental peoples on whom [the Americans] could rely,[15] he rejected the policy of re-unification and accepted the actual division of the country. He favoured, however, the merging of the Western zones, which would bring 'immediate economic and political benefits and potentially great military advantages.'[16]

Events moved swiftly in 1947. On 1 January the British and US zones were combined. In March the Truman Doctrine was proclaimed, thus ensuring the failure of the Moscow Conference. The chief result of the conference was, according to Clay, 'to convince the three foreign ministers representing the Western Powers of the intransigence of the Soviet position'. This led them to work more closely together in the future.[17] In June Marshall announced his plan for European recovery. Preparing the aid programme, Kennan declared: '. . . it is imperatively urgent today that the improvement of economic conditions and the revival of productive capacity in the west of Germany be made the primary object of our policy . . . and be given top priority.'[18] The American policy was supported wholeheartedly by the British and gradually the French also realized that the unification of Germany was no longer feasible.

In February 1948 the three powers held a conference on Western Germany. The resultant communiqué stated that they had agreed 'that close co-operation should be established among themselves . . . in all matters arising out of the ERP [Marshall Aid] in relation to Western Germany. Such co-operation is essential if Western Germany is to make its full and proper contribution to European recovery.'[19] The Czechoslovak crisis encouraged even closer links between the Western powers. In March the Brussels Treaty Organization was established, whereby the British, the French and the Benelux countries agreed to help each other in the event of an attack on any one of them. On 11 June Senate Resolution 239 approving the 'association of the United States . . . with regional and other collective arrangements . . . based on continuous and effective self-help and mutual aid', was passed by

64 votes to 6. This clearly indicated the possibility of giving the Brussels Pact the necessary military support.[20] Also in June, the USA and the Brussels Pact countries indicated that they intended to go ahead with the formation of a West German government. 'In the long run,' comments Ambrose, 'this could only mean that the West intended to merge West Germany into the proposed anti-Soviet military organization.'[21]

Such was the background to the Berlin crisis. Its immediate cause was the currency reform initiated by the Western powers. Some change was clearly needed. 'On the eve of the currency reform in the three western zones one cigarette cost twenty-five marks, a pound of coffee 1,500 marks. The monthly income of a worker or clerk varied between 300 and 400 marks a month.'[22] Under such conditions normal economic life was impossible. On 20 June a new currency, the Deutsche Mark, was introduced into the Western zones. The old Reichsmark was no longer valid: savings and bank holdings were reduced to 6·50 Deutsche Marks for every 100 Reichsmarks.[23] It was a necessary first step for the revival of the economy of Western Germany. Sokolovsky, the Soviet Military Governor, condemned it as 'a breach of the Potsdam decisions'. He also warned that: 'The prerequisites for free passenger traffic and goods traffic between the occupation zones will be destroyed.'[24] On 23 June the Russians, themselves disregarding the Potsdam protocol, announced a currency reform for the Soviet zone and for Greater Berlin. The Western governments refused to allow a new currency, over which they had no control, to circulate in their sectors of the city. Accordingly, they decided to introduce the Deutsche Mark into West Berlin. The Soviets replied by cutting communications between West Berlin and the Western zones. Thus began the blockade of Berlin.[25]

Access to the city by road, rail and canal was blocked. The air corridors remained open, however, and the British and Americans defeated the blockade by the Airlift. Round-the-clock missions into Berlin, supplying at their peak 13,000 tons of goods per day, provided the necessities of life for some $2\frac{1}{2}$ million people. On 12 May 1949 Stalin conceded defeat by lifting the blockade.

The conventional Western explanation of the episode is that Stalin was following his usual expansionist policy. In the words of Fischer: 'The Berlin blockade was a major Moscow bid – the last – to take over Europe'.[26] We have already seen that Soviet military aggression was most unlikely. It might be added here that in February 1948 Stalin had made the following comment to the Yugoslavs about the Greek Civil War, which was still dragging on: 'What, do you think that Great Britain and the United States – the United States, the most powerful state in the world – will permit you to break their line of communication in the Mediterranean? Nonsense . . . The uprising in Greece must be stopped, and as quickly as possible.'[27] It was not the language of a man prepared to challenge the Americans in Western Europe.

In the summer of 1948 the Soviets themselves were being challenged on a number of fronts. As well as the growing cohesion of the Western powers there was the challenge of Tito, about whose role in Greece Stalin had shown such anxiety. 'Soviet foreign policy, based on an occupied and divided Germany, a weakened Western Europe, and tight control of Eastern Europe, faced total collapse . . . the security of the Soviet Union itself now seemed threatened . . . The victor in the war was being hemmed in by the West, with the vanquished [Germany] playing a key role in the new coalition. Worst of all was the Western listening-post and outpost in the heart of the Soviet security belt, the Western sector in Berlin.'[28] It seems probable that the Berlin blockade was, in

Loading coal in the Berlin airlift.

Deutscher's phrase, a 'desperate gamble'[29] to save something from the wreckage; a somewhat despairing effort to delay the emergence of a western-oriented West German state.

Of course, following so closely after the Czech *coup*, it convinced many doubters in the West that the Soviet Union was indeed an expansionist power. 'The blockade,' noted Fleming, 'had provided grist to all the mills of anti-Russian propaganda; and the American and British peoples, outraged by Stalin's action, acclaimed their government for the reversal of alliances, the very idea of which had until quite recently been abhorrent to them.'[30] With the support of public opinion, both governments hastened to create a new anti-Soviet bloc.

During the summer of 1948 there were discussions between the Americans and the Brussels Pact countries. In December, the governments of Canada, Denmark, Iceland, Italy, Norway and Portugal were invited to join the new alliance. Dean Acheson, one of its main architects, became Secretary of State in January 1949. Truman, triumphantly re-elected, pledged in his Inaugural Address aid to European nations willing to defend themselves. On 4 April 1949 the North Atlantic Treaty was signed in Washington. The US Senate ratified it by a vote of 82 to 13 on 21 July.

A new era had begun.[31] Determined to halt Communist expansion, the United States committed itself to an entangling alliance. It had undertaken, for the first time in its history, the close military collaboration that Churchill had urged in his Fulton speech. For the next twenty years its allies (including authoritarian Portugal) could claim American assistance in preserving the *status quo*. Although circumstances might alter, the American obligation to NATO remained binding. The US response to any change in the balance of power became almost as inflexible as its attitude towards the Soviet Union.[32]

This revolution in American foreign policy had its critics. There were attacks from the right and the left. The conservative Senator Taft disliked the obligation of the USA to fight in defence of any member of NATO regardless of the circumstances.[33] The liberal Wallace opposed the treaty because it helped to harden the division of Europe into two hostile camps. He argued that the consequence of a military alliance was likely to be war, which would cost millions of American lives and bring the end of the American system.[34] However, the great majority of senators supported the involvement of the USA in the Western alliance. Like many other Americans, they shared the view of Secretary Acheson that only a strong United States stood 'between the Kremlin and dominion over the entire world'.[35]

The NATO treaty came into effect on 24 August 1949. Some ten days previously the first West German Parliament had been elected. Konrad Adenauer, leader of the Christian Democratic Party and a staunch anti-Communist, became Chancellor of the new Federal Republic.[36] Within a month the provisional People's Chamber in Berlin elected Wilhelm Pieck as President of the new state on the other side of the iron curtain, the German Democratic Republic.[37]

Thus a solution of sorts had been found for the German problem, which was the most crucial in Europe. There were two German states, each created in their own image by the two principal antagonists in the Cold War. For the next few years there were to be no serious alarms in Europe. The Cold War did not, however, peter out: the centre of conflict moved from Europe to Asia. While Germany was being divided, in China, for the first time in living memory, a government was imposing its authority over the whole country. On 1 October the Chinese Communists proclaimed the inauguration of the People's Republic of China.

Seven

THE COLD WAR IN ASIA

The victory of the Chinese Communists caused some Americans to refurbish the conspiracy theory of history which had, for example, interpreted the Greek Civil War as a Red plot. The theory was now applied to Asia, where the takeover in China was seen as a response to the setting up of NATO and the overt commitment of American troops in Europe. Stalin, having been denied control of the whole of Germany, had contrived to become master of China. We have seen that Truman was sure that the Soviets were out to rule the world. Here seemingly, was justification for his belief and for the tough policies that had flowed from it.

In fact the defeat of Chiang Kai-shek owed virtually nothing to Stalin: the revolution in China in 1949 was a purely Chinese affair. It was the culmination of a civil war that had been waged since 1927, when Chiang had tried to wipe out Communism in China. Quite correctly he felt that, so long as the Chinese Communists were active, his own position would be threatened. Until he was forced to flee from China (and since then also) his first priority was their destruction.[1] At times he came close to success but even five years before he was finally defeated it was clear that his régime was doomed. During the Second World War there was an uneasy truce between Chiang and the Communists, while China and the Western powers were fighting the Japanese. At that time Americans in China began to realize how precarious his position was. In November 1944 an American official informed the State Department: 'Relying upon his dispirited, shambling legions, his decadent, corrupt bureaucracy . . . and such nervous foreign support as he can muster, the Generalissimo may . . . plunge China into civil war. He cannot succeed . . . The Communists are already too strong for him . . . Chiang's feudal China cannot long exist alongside a dynamic popular government in north China. The Communists are in China to stay. And China's destiny is not

Mao Tse-tung leading the Peking victory parade which celebrated the establishment of the People's Republic of China.

Chiang's but theirs.'[2]

That was the view of most China experts in the State Department. However, the American government, ignoring their advice, supported Chiang when the civil war did break out once more. Between 1946 and 1949 he received hundreds of millions of dollars in aid and almost all his military equipment was American. Lavish aid was, however, ineffective against the hostility of the Chinese masses. Chiang's Kuomintang Party had failed utterly to tackle China's problems. In particular it had been unwilling to curb the power of the landlords and had thus forfeited the support of the most potent force in the country, the peasantry. It was precisely that force that the Communists had won over to their side. When Chiang retreated to Formosa few in China mourned his defeat.[3]

It was, however, a blow to many Americans. They found it hard to believe that all their dollars and their concern for a 'democratic' China could have been so unavailing. Acheson had tried to explain away the unhappy event in a paper published in August 1949. It stated: 'The unfortunate but inescapable fact is that the ominous result of the civil war in China was beyond the control of the government of the United States . . . It was the product of internal Chinese forces, forces which this country tried to influence but could not. A decision was arrived at within China, if only a decision by default.'[4] This realistic view did not commend itself to the critics of the Democratic Administration. For seventeen years the Republican Party in the United States had been in the political wilderness. It was ready to use any weapon to discredit the Democrats, especially since it had unexpectedly lost the presidential election in November 1948. One of its most powerful weapons emerged early in 1950 – the junior senator for Wisconsin, Joseph McCarthy.

McCarthy, realizing that anti-Communism was a popular issue in the United States, saw that he could advance his own career and weaken the Democrats by persisting with the charge that they were 'soft on Communism'. As we have seen, the Truman Administration had in fact taken a tough line with the Russians (as well as with many Americans) and it was generally felt that in Europe the Communist 'offensive' had been effectively halted. McCarthy's campaign began, however, after the Communist takeover in China. That, he alleged, had been facilitated by traitors in the State Department. In February 1950 he claimed that 205 of its employees were known to be members of the Communist Party.[5] His ludicrous charges seemingly panicked the usually urbane Acheson who dramatically revised the official version of the China débâcle. Instead of insisting on the historically correct explanation given in the State Department paper, he sought to parry McCarthy's attacks by suggesting that everything was the fault of the Russians. The familiar bogeymen of the Kremlin were to come to the rescue of the Truman Administration. Thus, a week after McCarthy first made his false allegations, Acheson

Senator Joseph McCarthy with the Press.

put forward his new interpretation: 'The Communists [the Russian variety] took over China at a ridiculously small cost. What they did was to invite some Chinese leaders who were dissatisfied with the way things were going in their country to come to Moscow. There they thoroughly indoctrinated them so that they returned to China prepared to resort to any means whatsoever to establish Communist control. They were completely subservient to the Moscow régime . . . These agents then mingled among the people and sold them on the personal material advantages of Communism . . .'[6]

According to that farrago of nonsense China had gone Red only because of a Kremlin-hatched conspiracy. If someone else had 'sold them on the personal material advantages' of capitalism, the Chinese might not have turned Communist. Perhaps if the USA had spent $4 billion instead of a mere $2 billion Chiang Kai-shek might still be in control. The lesson drawn was that America must spend more on 'security', which meant appropriating enormous sums for weapons and armies.

In April 1950 a committee of government officials produced a document, to be known as NSC-68 (National Security Council paper No. 68), which attempted to forecast the policy required in the new situation.[7] Prescribing the best line of action for the USA, the document said: 'It can strike out on a bold and massive program of rebuilding the West's defensive potential to surpass that of the Soviet world, and of meeting each fresh challenge promptly and unequivocally.' Commenting on the implication of such a strategy, the authors warned: 'This means virtual abandonment by the United States of trying to distinguish between national and global security. It also means the end of subordinating security needs to the traditional budgeting restrictions; of asking, "How much security can we afford?" In other words, security must henceforth become the dominant element in the national budget, and other elements must be accommodated to it.' Naturally, this would cost a great deal of money: 'This new concept of the security needs of the nation calls for annual appropriations of the order of $50 billion, or not much below the former wartime levels.' The appropriation when the document was produced was $13 billion.

It is significant that such huge increases in armaments spending were suggested even before the outbreak of the Korean War. Indeed at the time NSC-68 was published some kind of balance of power had been established in Europe. Except in the minds of those who saw Mao Tse-tung simply as Stalin's puppet, the Russians had made no overt move to disturb the balance elsewhere in the world. In September 1949 the Soviets had, it is true, exploded an atomic bomb some years ahead of the time expected by the Americans. However, that event did not so much pose a threat to the United States as remove one from the Soviet Union.[8] According to some Americans it made agreement on the control of atomic weapons more imperative. Given the stabilization in Europe, it gave a new incentive to the search for an accommodation between the two super-powers. 'In early 1950 there was undoubtedly a feeling among "millions of Americans that there must be a new approach to the Soviet Union in order to close the horrible vistas" ahead. The time for a real effort to stop the Cold War seemed urgently present.'[9]

This feeling found no echo, however, in Acheson. He refused to 'negotiate from weakness' and in March called for a policy of

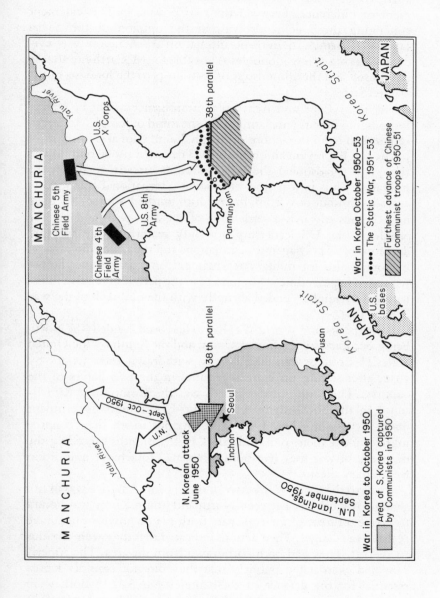

War in Korea October 1950–53

••••• The Static War, 1951–53

////// Furthest advance of Chinese communist troops 1950–51

MANCHURIA

Yalu River

Chinese 5th Field Army

U.S. X Corps

Chinese 4th Field Army

U.S. 8th Army

38th parallel

Panmunjom

Korea Strait

JAPAN

War in Korea to October 1950

Area of S.Korea captured by Communists in 1950

MANCHURIA

Yalu River

U.N. Sept–Oct 1950

N.Korean attack June 1950

38th parallel

Seoul

Inchon

U.N. landings September 1950

Pusan

Korea Strait

JAPAN

U.S. bases

'total diplomacy'. This, in effect, meant presenting to the Russians a series of demands as preconditions for the negotiation of a settlement of differences between the two powers.[10] The statement containing those demands was, in the opinion of the *Soviet Literary Gazette*, 'an insolent ultimatum'.[11] Acheson was evidently leaving as few loopholes as possible for McCarthyite attacks on himself and the administration as traitors to the interests of the United States.[12]

Indeed NSC-68 and Acheson's intransigence might be seen as responses to threats emanating from the mind of Joseph McCarthy rather than from the actions of Joseph Stalin. Global security must be the aim to prevent another China. The cost must be borne, even though it quadrupled the large amounts already spent on the military. 'Thus in a period of relative international tranquillity, amidst admonitions from many distinguished sources to open negotiations towards a settlement of the European and nuclear problems, the US leadership not only reaffirmed the strategic decisions of 1945–7 against negotiations and the use of diplomacy, but opted also for military rearmament on a scale never before witnessed in peacetime.'[13] In June 1950 the period of relative international tranquillity ended abruptly with the outbreak of the war in Korea.

After the Second World War Korea had been divided: the North being occupied by the Soviet Union and the South by the United States.[14] Both powers had largely withdrawn their troops by 1950, after setting up Korean régimes in the two halves of the country. The leader in the North was the Communist Kim Il-sung; in the South there was an anti-Communist government under Syngman Rhee. Both were anxious to see their country unified under their own leadership. In the months preceding the outbreak of war they had both threatened to achieve unification by military means.[15]

By 1950 the Cold War between Russia and America was in full swing. Any conflict between North and South Korea was bound to create a threat of general war. Both major powers must have realized the danger. Their actions indicated that they were anxious to avert it. They had both withdrawn from the area. The Americans had even stated publicly that they did not consider Korea essential for the defence of their interests in Asia.[16] Both were seemingly caught unawares when war came. These facts might suggest that it started because Rhee and Kim Il-sung were no longer prepared to tolerate a divided nation; that North and South provoked each other until one of them launched a major offensive; that it was in origin a civil war. That was not, however, the version that gained acceptance in the West. In Washington there was no doubt that it was Stalin who had taken the decision to launch the North Koreans against the South. The opinion of the well-known commentators, the Alsop brothers, was that 'the Kremlin has clearly and consciously risked a world war.'[17] In other words the Soviets were once again trying to extend their empire.

Evidence about the origin of the Korean War is largely circumstantial. The orthodox assessment in the West of the circumstances is that the North Koreans could not conceivably have started the war without consulting Stalin. In fact, when they attacked across the border on 25 June, they were, it is argued, following orders from Moscow. Stalin, having lost the initiative in Europe was determined to regain it in Asia. China, now in Communist hands, was an excellent base for further offensives. Deutscher indeed has suggested that Stalin, in pursuing a forward policy in Korea, was demonstrating that the Chinese were not the only Communists in Asia.[18] He was not going to be upstaged by Mao. By taking over the whole of Korea he would be threatening the American control of Japan, one of the key areas of US strategy in the Pacific. A success in Korea might also encourage the Communists fighting in Indochina. (At the beginning of 1950 the USA was sufficiently concerned about the French position there to grant them $10 million credits.)[19] It seemed obvious that the war had been instigated, for a number of reasons, by the Russians. Korea was yet another piece in the jigsaw of Soviet expansionism. That version was (and still is) accepted by majority opinion in the West. A minority, however, has argued that other circumstantial evidence makes the conventional version less credible.

At the time the war began the Russians had walked out of the Security Council of the United Nations. They were thus unable to exercise their veto when the Americans began to organize intervention in the Korean War by United Nations' forces. Was it likely that the Machiavellian Stalin would have ignored such a possibility?[20] Furthermore, why should the Soviets risk a war when the régime in South Korea seemed in imminent danger of collapse? In the month preceding the war Rhee's government had been heavily defeated in the elections. The results reflected the widespread disillusionment with the repressive apparatus of Rhee's police state.[21] It was a situation eminently exploitable by the North Koreans without any major military move. Even Acheson later admitted that 'the Communists had far from exhausted the potentialities for obtaining their objectives through guerrilla and psychological warfare, political pressure and intimidation.'[22] In such circumstances it is perhaps remarkable that Stalin should run the risk of provoking America by open hostilities.

I. F. Stone contends that it was not Stalin but Syngman Rhee who precipitated the war.[23] Abetted by Chiang Kai-shek, General MacArthur and some US officials he deliberately provoked an attack from the North in order to force the American government to extend its containment policy to the whole Pacific area. Without American support both South Korea and Formosa (Chiang's retreat) were extremely vulnerable to Communist pressure. One way to obtain such support was to threaten the balance of power in Asia, hence the war. 'It should not be forgotten,' says Stone, 'that in this, as in any other unsolved crime, it is useful to begin by determining who benefited.'[24] Stone's argument is that the war's main beneficiaries, Rhee and Chiang, were also its instigators: 'The hypothesis that invasion was encouraged politically by silence, invited militarily by defensive formations, and finally set off by some minor lunges across the border when all was ready would explain a great deal.'[25] In support of Stone's conspiracy theory, Horowitz points out that '. . . MacArthur's whole subsequent course of behaviour (and that of his powerful supporters) was consistent with a strategy designed to provoke and then escalate a war in Asia.'[26]

We might mention two other accounts of the war's origin. Harrison Salisbury argues that Stalin was responsible but that his objective was not 'a weakening of the US posture in the Pacific'. It was to threaten 'a man whose philosophy and tactics were anathema to him and who . . . had come to power in the greatest nation of Asia, the nation with whom Russia had the longest frontier . . .'[27] In other words – Mao Tse-tung. 'Far from Korea representing a collaboration of the two Communist giants against the West it actually represented Stalin's daring power squeeze against his supposed ally.'[28] There is a strong suggestion of hindsight in this version, which was put forward after Chinese and Soviet troops had clashed at various points on their long frontier.

Yet another account has appeared in the memoirs attributed to Khrushchev: 'The North Koreans wanted to give a helping hand to their brethren who were under the heel of Syngman Rhee. Stalin persuaded Kim Il-sung that he should think it over . . . Kim . . . returned to Moscow when he had worked everything out . . . Stalin had his doubts. He was worried that the Americans would jump in, but we were inclined that if the war were fought swiftly – and Kim Il-sung was sure that it could be won swiftly – then intervention by the USA could be avoided. Nevertheless, Stalin decided to ask Mao Tse-tung's opinion . . . I must stress that the war wasn't Stalin's idea, but Kim Il-sung's. Kim was the initiator. Stalin, of course didn't try to dissuade him. . . . Mao Tse-tung also answered affirmatively . . . and put forward the opinion that the USA would not intervene since the war would be an internal matter which the Korean people would decide for themselves.'[29] This is an interesting statement but cannot be accepted without question. In the first place, the authenticity of the memoirs has not been established incontrovertibly. Secondly, even if the words are Khrushchev's they are not corroborated.

Until the appropriate files are made public it will not be possible to say definitely who started the Korean War. The military evidence, which is substantial, indicates that it was indeed launched by the North Koreans. They were certainly well prepared. In June their army had seven divisions ready for combat, three others newly activated, two independent regiments, an armoured brigade and five brigades of a paramilitary border constabulary. Their troops were well trained and supported by artillery and powerful T-34 tanks. To provide air cover there were 150–200 aircraft, mainly Yak fighters and Ilyushin ground attack bombers. By contrast the South Korean army had been inadequately trained and lacked heavy artillery, tanks and aircraft.[30] By the end of June, a mere week after hostilities began, over half the army of the South had been destroyed. The Americans on the spot were ill-equipped to retrieve the situation: the four infantry divisions of the US Eighth Army, based in Japan, were at 70 percent of their established strength.[31] Such facts hardly suggest that the North was provoked to attack. Rather they point to a deliberate concentration of power by Kim Il-sung to smash the southern forces. The unreadiness of the American troops in Japan must make us question the notion that MacArthur connived at a Northern offensive which threatened to engulf the South in a matter of weeks. Furthermore, if Rhee did provoke that offensive it is remarkable that in the last twenty years no evidence of his provocation has come to light. On those grounds we may conclude that the North Koreans moved first. The question whether they acted on their own initiative or followed orders from the Kremlin remains open.[32]

As Horowitz notes: 'Whatever the war's immediate origin, it is clear that fundamentally it was a civil war in which foreign powers eventually became deeply involved.'[33] The day after war began the British *Manchester Guardian* commented: 'The invasion is a classic type of incident which endangers world peace when the world is divided into two camps. The procedure for dealing with it is also familiar from past experience. The objectives are the cessation of hostilities, withdrawal of troops, and above all, the exclusion of the Great Powers from the conflict. These must be the aims of the Security Council.'[34] At first the US did avoid involvement. Then on 27 June, two days after the fighting began, Truman issued a statement committing the USA to military intervention against any further expansion of Communist rule in the Pacific area. He also promised increased military aid to Indochina and the Philippines, and ordered US air and sea forces to give cover and support to the Korean government troops. On the same day the UN Security Council, under the strongest pressure from America, passed a resolution recommending that 'members of the United Nations furnish such assistance to the Republic of Korea as may be necessary to repel the armed attack and to restore international peace and security in the area.'[35] Thus the unilateral action by the USA was justified, after the event, by the UN. On 7 July the UN passed another resolution which effectively gave control of its forces to General MacArthur, with the weak proviso that the US should provide the Security Council with 'reports as appropriate on the course of action taken under the unified command'. This carte blanche to MacArthur was to have the gravest consequences.[36]

Immediately after the war started there was a drastic reversal of American policy in the Far East. In place of the concept of limited defence there was an unlimited commitment to extend

US support, military and economic, throughout the Pacific area. This included the 'neutralization' of Formosa, which meant using the Seventh Fleet to safeguard from Red Chinese attacks an island previously regarded as unnecessary for the strategic defence of America. The new policy was in effect an extension of the Truman Doctrine to the whole of Asia.[37] This might seem an exaggerated response to what in many ways was a civil war in a minor Asiatic country. On the very day when Truman announced the policy changes, the US implicitly recognized that it was a civil war. Four hours after the President's statement, the State Department informed the press that the American ambassador in Moscow was to ask the Soviet Foreign Office to help to bring an end to the fighting in Korea. As Stone comments: 'The Truman announcement at noon rested on the implied conclusion that the events in Korea proved that "Moscow would now use military force to spread Communism". The announcement at 4 p.m. implied that the Korean conflict was a purely civil war which Russia might help to end.'[38]

A more important example of American inconsistency was the decision to extend the war to North Korea. At first the North Koreans swept all before them. Their offensive was however halted by the defence of Pusan and then by the landing behind their lines at Inchon, which was brilliantly organized by Mac-Arthur. On 30 September, some fifteen days after Inchon, the UN forces had reached the border on the Thirty-eighth Parallel and the North Koreans were in full flight. Thus the objectives of the UN resolutions had been achieved. The invasion had been repulsed and the way was open for a negotiated settlement. During the first three months of the war, neither Russia nor China became directly involved in it. Their behaviour indicated that they would be willing to see a return to the pre-war situation.[39]

It was hardly to be expected, however, that the victorious UN forces would be quite so keen to end the war on those terms. The enemy was on the run and there was a strong temptation to smash him so thoroughly that he would not threaten invasion again. On the part of Syngman Rhee there was an irresistible urge to reunity the country by force of arms, as he had threatened to do before 25 June. The Americans shared his attitude and, reversing their previous policy, decided to cross the parallel. On 1 October South Korean troops under MacArthur's command advanced across the border deep into North Korean territory. Six days later the UN General Assembly belatedly approved the invasion.[40] Thereafter it was no longer possible to claim that the UN forces were in Korea solely to check aggression. Clearly, they were being used to destroy North Korea: 'they were no longer acting as police, but as co-belligerents on the side of the South Koreans.'[41]

The most important result of this action was China's involvement in the war. At the time the American leaders claimed that there was no reason to expect Chinese intervention. The Chinese, they claimed, had nothing to fear from an extension of the war to North Korea: the UN forces had no designs on Manchuria, no plans to attack China.[42] The same leaders had, of course, said that the US was fighting in Korea 'solely for the purpose of restoring the Republic of Korea to its status prior to the invasion from the north'.[43] They had changed their minds when it suited them. Furthermore, the UN forces were commanded by a man who had publicly proclaimed his admiration of Chiang Kai-shek and his hostility towards Red China.[44] Stone has suggested a parallel situation which may help us to understand why the Chinese were so apprehensive. 'Let Americans think for a moment,' he says, 'how they would react if the armies of another great power from across the seas were crushing a Mexican government friendly to the USA, strafing Texas border towns, and operating under a general who threatened war against the USA itself.'[45] We might, through this analogy, begin to feel that China's involvement in the war was caused by genuine fears about American intentions. A study made by the RAND corporation for the US Air Force in 1960 indicated that the Chinese decision to enter the war was indeed 'rationally motivated'.[46] Snow points out that: 'It was not implemented in combat until four months after the outbreak of hostilities – not until Mr Truman had received two warnings from Peking against sending troops north of the Thirty-eighth Parallel, and not until American (and UN) forces were hard upon China's frontier on the Yalu River, which American planes were bombing.'[47]

By the end of November the Chinese had openly intervened on the side of the North Koreans.[48] Within a month influential Americans were demanding that China be branded an aggressor! Nehru, the Premier of India, warned that such an action would 'bolt and bar the door to a peaceful settlement in the Far East.'[49]

Nevertheless, on 30 January 1951 the United States dragooned the UN into passing the appropriate resolution.[50]

More than twenty years were to elapse before China was eventually allowed to become a member of the United Nations. Meanwhile relations between the USA and China were as hostile as if they were at war. For two years, until the Korean armistice was signed in 1953, the Americans and Chinese were indeed fighting each other. Only the determination of Truman and the Chinese leaders averted a full scale conflict betwen the two powers. Until his dismissal in April 1951, MacArthur did his utmost to precipitate a war between them.[51] Public opinion in the United States was much more inclined to support MacArthur's view that the Korean War could not be won without attacking Manchuria, which would undoubtedly have increased the chances of a Third World War.[52]

Although that ultimate disaster was avoided, the Cold War, nevertheless, reached a new level of intensity. The United States, already the self-appointed policeman of Europe, became policeman for the whole world. Truman ensured that the policeman was well armed. 'He got emergency powers from Congress to expedite war mobilization, made selective service a permanent feature of American life, submitted a $50 billion defense budget that followed the guidelines of NSC-68, sent two more divisions (a total of six) to Europe, doubled the number of air groups to 95, obtained new bases in Morocco, Libya, and Saudi Arabia, increased the Army by 50 percent to 3.5 million men, pushed forward the Japanese peace treaty, stepped up aid to the French in Indochina, initiated the process of adding Greece and Turkey to NATO and began discussions with Franco which led to American aid to Fascist Spain in return for military bases there.'[53]

The price of preparedness was the militarization of the United States. Millis, himself a supporter of the Cold War, pointed out that Truman's administration created 'an enormously expanded military establishment, beyond anything we had ever contemplated in time of peace . . . It evoked a huge and apparently permanent armaments industry, now wholly dependent . . . on government contracts. The Department of Defense had become without question the biggest industrial management operation in the world, the great private operations, like General Motors, du Pont, the leading airplane manufacturers . . . had assumed positions of monopoly power which . . . seemed to raise new questions as to the legal and constitutional organization of the state.'⁵⁴

On China, too, the Korean War made a great impact. For acting in self-defence, in its own opinion, it had been called an aggressor and publicly humiliated by the world's foremost international organization. This happened when the Chinese, after decades of struggle, had at last begun to regain their self-respect as a nation. At a critical time they were turned in on themselves. Much has been written about the bamboo curtain, behind which the Chinese isolated themselves from the rest of the world. It is often forgotten that the isolation was forced upon them. What cut them off from outside contacts was not so much their own ideology as their exclusion from UNO and the ring of bases established round their borders by the United States.★ Feeling threatened, the Chinese replied by taking up threatening attitudes themselves. Their uncompromising hostility to the capitalist world, in turn, seemed to justify the policies that had helped to create it. It gave credence to the US fear of a monolithic Communist bloc stretching from the River Elbe to the China Sea.

★ 'The concrete expression of the policy of containment with hostility was a series of alliances ringing China: with Japan, Australia, New Zealand, South Korea, Formosa, and finally the setting up of the South-East Asia Treaty Organization.' Schurmann and Schell, *Communist China* (Penguin) p. 293.

Eight

THE TENSION EASES

When he left office in January 1953 Truman could claim that he had successfully contained the Communists in Europe and Asia. His Republican opponents were unimpressed. During the election campaign of 1952, which ended in victory for Eisenhower, they damned containment as 'negative, futile and immoral', since it abandoned 'countless human beings to a despotism and Godless terrorism'.[1] John Foster Dulles, who was to become the new Secretary of State, warned the electors: 'The only way to stop a head-on collision with the Soviet Union is to break it up from within.'[2] In his first official speech, in January 1953, he declared: 'To all those suffering under Communist slavery . . . let us say: you can count on us.'[3] The Eisenhower Administration, it seemed, was going to roll back the atheistic tide and liberate the slaves in Asia and Eastern Europe.

In June 1953 a workers' uprising in Eastern Germany, precipitated by reduced wages and increased work norms, exposed the Republican rhetoric. Demonstrations in Leipzig spread to Berlin and other cities. The government crushed the rebellion with Soviet tanks. Western notes of protest were ignored and the new Soviet régime, which had been considering withdrawing from East Germany, abruptly reversed its policy. As Deutscher put it: '. . . the East Germans hoped that their "direct action" would speed up the collapse of the Pieck–Ulbricht régime, which in early June looked as if it had already been half-dismantled. The result achieved was the direct opposite: the revolt compelled the Kremlin to prop up the . . . régime in the most spectacular and demonstrative manner.'[4] Thus the theory that the Soviet system could be broken up 'from within' was badly dented.

Shortly before the uprising, Dulles had said: '. . . those who do not believe that results can be accomplished by moral pressures, by the weight of propaganda, just do not know what they are talking about'.[5] Moral pressure having failed, however, he pro-

Secretary of State, John Foster Dulles.

duced a new plan. Liberation, or 'rollback', would, he argued, be feasible if it were supported by a capacity for 'massive retaliation' by nuclear weapons. Such a policy would have the extra merit of being cheaper than the Democratic programme of containment. Instead of building up large conventional forces, the USA could place 'more reliance on deterrent power'. The Communists would not dare to take advantage of the situation on the ground because of the threat of nuclear bombs which could be dropped at any time by the US Strategic Air Force, which was constantly on the alert. Continually thwarted in their expansionist aims, the Communists would be forced to grant freedom to their slaves. 'If we can deter such aggression as would mean general war . . . then we can let time and fundamentals work for us . . . We intend that our conduct and example shall continue, as in the past, to show all men how good can be the fruits of freedom.'[6]

It is perhaps remarkable that Dulles could advance such a theory when freedom in the USA was being eroded by the squalid manipulations of McCarthy. However, he was unaware of any inconsistency. 'If,' he continued, 'we persist in the courses I outline we shall confront dictatorship with a task that is, in the long run, beyond its strength. For unless it changes, it must suppress the human desires that freedom satisfies – as we shall be demonstrating. If the dictators persist in their present course, then it is they who will be limited to superficial successes, while their foundation crumbles under the tread of their iron boots . . .'[7]

The theory of massive retaliation was based on the American hydrogen bomb which had been successfully tested in November 1952. Dulles made the speech just quoted in January 1954. Five months previously, in August 1953, the Russians had also exploded a hydrogen bomb. Dulles believed that he could use America's nuclear capacity to win the Cold War. He refused to recognize that the development of the Soviet H-bomb created conditions not of victory but of stalemate or mutual destruction. Hydrogen bombs were 250 times more powerful than the 'primitive' devices dropped on Hiroshima and Nagasaki. It would soon be possible for the United States and the Soviet Union to destroy each other.[8] The choice was not between victory and defeat but between annihilation and co-existence. The reality of nuclear stalemate made victory illusory. It was hard for some Americans to accept this. Their early monopoly of atomic weapons had distorted their judgment. They had, it is true, been obliged to recognize the limitations of such weapons and the Russian A-bomb had destroyed some illusions. However, US technology had triumphed again with the H-bomb and had reinforced American nuclear superiority. To acknowledge that Soviet technology had once more caught up with them and that the Russians were visibly approaching nuclear parity with them was not easy. In the opinion of Horowitz: 'Dulles never acknowledged it.'[9]

Fleming has pointed out that Americans 'discounted Soviet science and industry far too heavily.'[10] The fact was that, for years, the Soviets had concentrated great resources on the task of breaking the US atomic monopoly. In 1956 Blackett commented: 'With our present knowledge there can be little doubt that for many years past an important element in Stalin's policy was to attempt to impose co-existence on the West by achieving atomic parity. This was, in fact, achieved within six months of Stalin's death – for the first Soviet H-bomb in August 1953 can be considered as signifying the success of the policy.'[11]

Lane has commented that 'when Soviet strategic interest is at stake, radical ideological shifts can be made to suit immediate policy . . . and the self-interest of the USSR is a most important determinant of Soviet policy'.[12] This may help to substantiate Blackett's claim that Stalin was striving 'to impose co-existence on the West', a policy which was clearly in contradiction to the Leninist principle that clashes between the Soviet Republic and bourgeois states were inevitable. The fact was that Lenin himself had ignored it when it seemed necessary to do so for the sake of the revolution. Stalin followed suit, not so much for the cause of the revolution as in the interest of Soviet security. Deutscher points out that 'in his essay on "Economic Problems" published in 1952, he went on record with the view that wars between the imperialist powers and the countries of socialism were no longer "inevitable"'.[13] Paradoxically, it was by providing Russia with nuclear weapons that Stalin created the conditions for a policy of co-existence. As Blackett says: 'In so far . . . as the present *détente* is a result of the present Soviet leaders' confidence in their strength it is as a result not of Stalin's death but of the ruthless methods by which he drove his country to the scientific, technological and industrial efforts without which atomic parity would have been long delayed.'[14]

There was in fact greater continuity in Soviet policy after Stalin's death, on 5 March 1953, than is often recognized. Even under Stalin it was never so rigid as Dulles, for example, imagined it to be. 'It is a mistake,' says Deutscher, 'to see Soviet policy as static, fixed, and closed in itself. The behaviour of Soviet diplomacy is, of course, affected by controversies and alignments within the ruling group and by many domestic pressures and even more so by foreign ones. The changing balance of those pressures is reflected in the pattern of diplomatic moves. In a critical period that balance changes more swiftly than in normal times. Soviet foreign policy since Stalin's death has at times been like a see-saw in full swing.'[15] At one end of the see-saw were the old-style Stalinists such as Molotov. Throughout his long career he had been concerned about the vulnerability of the Soviet Union. Hostile groupings of capitalist powers had, in his experience, constantly threatened its security and at times its very existence. Suspicion of the West was part of his nature.[16] At the other end were those who, like Malenkov, thought that it was in the interest of the Soviet Union to seek some kind of *détente* with the West. Shortly after he became Prime Minister Malenkov declared: 'There is no disputed or outstanding issue at the present time which cannot be settled peacefully on the basis of mutual agreement of the countries concerned. This refers to our relations with all States, including those with the United States.'[17]

Under Stalin's successors co-existence became a major aspect of Soviet foreign policy, although it was always viewed suspiciously by the hard-liners in the Soviet hierarchy. One of the first fruits of the new approach was the Korean Armistice in July 1953. Talks had been dragging on for two years and both sides had created difficulties. Finally they agreed that the Thirty-eighth Parallel should continue to be the dividing line between North and South. Of course the armistice was not simply the consequence of greater flexibility in the Kremlin. The pressure exerted by the new American administration was probably more important. Dulles had indeed threatened to use atomic weapons to force a settlement on the Chinese.[18] He did not see the armistice as evidence of a more conciliatory Soviet attitude. To him it was a victory for his policy of massive retaliation, this time against the Chinese. Confrontation, not co-existence, was his watchword. This was shown clearly in his handling of the situation in Indochina.

Since 1946 there had been a war there between Vietnamese nationalists, under the leadership of the Communist Ho Chi Minh, and the French who were trying to re-impose their colonial rule.[19] At first the USA had been neutral. Its attitude changed sharply with the victory of Mao Tse-tung in October 1949. According to the account in the Pentagon Papers: 'After the fall of mainland China to the Chinese Communists, the Truman administration moved to support Emperor Bao Dai [a French puppet] and provide military aid to the French against the Communist-led Vietminh . . .' Thus, 'the course of US policy was set to block further Communist expansion in Asia . . . the United States thereafter was directly involved in the developing tragedy in Vietnam'.[20] By 1954 their aid programme amounted to \$1.1 billion and the US was paying for 78 percent of the cost of the war.[21]

In April 1954 Eisenhower proclaimed publicly the 'falling domino' theory that provided the rationale of American involvement. The theory had been put forward first in the National Security Council in February 1950. It assumed that the countries of Southeast Asia were like a row of dominoes. If one fell it would knock down the next in line and so on, until they had all fallen. In 1950 it was expressed thus: 'The neighbouring countries of Thailand and Burma could be expected to fall under Communist domination if Indochina is controlled by a Communist government. The balance of Southeast Asia would then be in grave hazard.'[22] The theory was elaborated in succeeding years. 'Subsequent Council decision papers throughout the nineteen-fifties repeated this formulation with ever-increasing sweep. A . . . paper approved by President Eisenhower in January 1954, predicted that the "loss of any single country" in Southeast Asia would ultimately lead to the loss of all Southeast Asia, then India and Japan, and finally "endanger the stability and security of Europe".'[23]

While Eisenhower was approving the NSC paper which stressed the importance of the war in Indochina, the outcome of the war itself was in doubt. Neither side seemed able to achieve victory. In April 1954 the Geneva Conference met to discuss 'the problem of restoring peace in Indochina'. Dulles proposed to solve the problem by US intervention to defeat the Communists. Even after the conference began he canvassed British support. Eden, the British Foreign Minister, 'told him . . . that if a settlement were achieved at the conference, the United Kingdom would be prepared to join in guaranteeing it. If the conference failed, we would be ready to examine the situation afresh, but we were not ready to take part in armed intervention now.'[24]

On 7 May 1954 the Vietminh won a decisive victory against the French at Dienbienphu. Most observers appreciated that it meant the end of the war. Dulles still hoped that American intervention might save the day. The French, however, had had enough of the war and by June the Americans too realized that 'the time for intervention had run out'.[25] In July agreement was reached at Geneva.

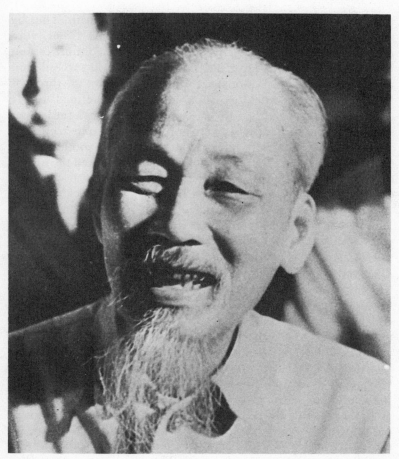

Ho Chi Minh leader of the Viet Minh and subsequently President of North Vietnam.

Vietnam was 'temporarily' divided at the Seventeenth Parallel. Elections were to be held within two years to decide whether Ho Chi Minh or his opponents should govern the whole country. According to the Pentagon historian: '. . . except for the United States, the major powers were satisfied with their handiwork.'[26] In America, however, the NSC felt that the settlement was 'a major forward stride of Communism which [could] lead to the loss of Southeast Asia'.[27] To counteract it, the United States should take over from France the task of giving military, economic and political backing to the government of South Vietnam. Thus by 1955 the USA were firmly supporting Ngo Dinh Diem, who refused to take part in the elections which would almost certain have given victory to Ho Chi Minh.[28] Dulles had succeeded in undermining the international agreements. 'Without the threat of US intervention, South Vietnam could not have refused to . . . discuss the elections called for . . . under the Geneva settlement without being immediately overrun by the Vietminh armies.'[29]

Dulles took an equally intransigent stance over another Asian crisis. In March 1955 the Chinese Communists attacked the islands of Quemoy and Matsu which, although they were just off the Chinese mainland, were occupied by Chiang Kai-shek's troops. Nehru, the Prime Minister of India, pointed out that it was 'almost generally recognized that those islands should immediately be evacuated and taken possession of by the Government of the mainland'.[30] The Americans, beguiled by their domino theory, disagreed. 'As the Chinese began to bombard Quemoy and Matsu, the Eisenhower administration seriously considered dropping nuclear weapons on the mainland.' Dulles threatened to use 'new and powerful weapons of precision, which can utterly destroy military targets' – in other words, tactical atomic bombs. Ambrose comments that: 'At no other time in the Cold War did the United States come so close to launching a preventive war.'[31] The Chinese gave way and the Dulles policy of brinkmanship, going to the brink of war to force the enemy to retreat, was triumphant.

'In the process, however,' as Ambrose says, 'it had scared the wits out of people around the globe . . . one American bomber carried more destructive power than all the explosives set off in all the world's history put together . . . The small, tactical atomic bombs Dulles was talking about were much larger than those dropped on Japan. Ever since the first American tests of the new fission bomb, Winston Churchill had been urging the United States and the Soviets to meet at the summit to try to resolve their differences. The Americans had consistently rejected his calls for a summit meeting, but by mid-1955, as the Russians began to improve both the size of their bombs and their delivery capabilities, and as the Formosa crisis made the United States face squarely the possibility of a nuclear exchange, Eisenhower and Dulles were more amenable.'[32]

There were indications that the Soviet leaders also were ready to

Nikita Khrushchev.

negotiate. In February 1955 they signed a peace treaty with Austria, despite Molotov's insistence at the Berlin Conference of 1954 that the Austrian treaty could be signed only at the same time as a treaty with Germany. Their change of mind is open to various inter- pretations.[33] One view is that the Soviets recognized that the new nuclear balance made their tenuous territorial influence in Austria less important. Furthermore, their toleration of neutrality in Europe might win over neutrals elsewhere, in the world. The following comment in a Soviet textbook seems to confirm that point: 'Austria's acceptance of neutrality serves as an example for

93

many other countries and shows that in the present international conditions even a small capitalist country which relies on the support of peace-loving powers can conduct an independent policy and abstain from participating in the blocs of imperialist powers.'[34]

Further evidence that the Soviets wanted a *détente* was provided by the visit of Khrushchev and other leaders to Yugoslavia eleven days after the signing of the Austrian treaty.[35] There was no obvious reason for the First Secretary of the Soviet Communist Party to abase himself before the heretical Tito. The Soviet Union was more powerful and secure than when Tito was denounced as a Western agent. What then were the reasons for the visit? To some extent the *rapprochement* with Yugoslavia was part of the process of abandoning the policies of Tito's enemy, Stalin. Recognizing that mistakes had been made, it indicated that powerful figures in the Soviet government were determined to take a new line. It was also yet another appeal to neutral opinion. Finally, it was, in some degree, a move away from the dogmatic pseudo-Marxism of Stalin to a more dialectical approach: a recognition that Tito, instead of being the arch-heretic was in fact trying to suit Marxist principles to the specific problems of Yugoslavia, as Lenin had adapted Marxism to the peculiar situation of Russia in 1917. In the month following the mission to Yugoslavia, Khrushchev attended the Summit Conference at Geneva.

During the summer of 1955 there seemed to be a mood of disenchantment with the Cold War. Ever since the death of Stalin there had been suggestions for a conference of the leaders of the major combatants in the Cold War. Churchill, in a remarkable reversal of his Fulton attitudes, had been advocating such a meeting since May 1953. It finally opened in July 1955. Those who foolishly expected a dramatic resolution of international problems were disappointed. No major changes ensued. However, after years of mud-slinging in public, the USA and the Soviet Union decided that their leaders could talk to each other again. In the circumstances it was, in itself, a major change. 'In Moscow, *Izvestia* headed its first post-Geneva editorial: "A New Era in International Relations Has Begun". Eisenhower was presented as a man who seeks peace . . . It was now clear that the Soviet leaders went to Geneva "seriously desirous of improving the international atmosphere".'[36]

The Soviet leaders were also proving to themselves that attempts at *détente* were not a betrayal of Soviet interests. According to the Khrushchev memoirs, Stalin expected the West to take advantage of his successors: 'Right up until his death Stalin used to tell us, "You'll see, when I'm gone the imperialistic powers will wring your necks like chickens".'[37] It was true that, apart from Molotov, the Russian leadership had little experience of foreign affairs. Inexperience might well have led to intransigence. After the Summit Conference, however, the new men felt more sure of themselves. Khrushchev's assessment was: 'We had established ourselves as able to hold our own in the international arena.'[38]

While the meeting boosted the confidence of the Soviet leaders, it undermined the uncompromising policies of the US Secretary of State. Brinkmanship was finished as was the notion of the liberation of Eastern Europe. The Western powers had in effect recognized that the Cold War could not be won; that a stalemate existed and that the *status quo* in Europe and China . . . had to be substantially accepted.[39]

Events in Moscow, however, were soon to shake the *status quo* in the Communist bloc.

Nine

CO-EXISTENCE AND CRISES

In February 1956 the Twentieth Congress of the Communist Party of the Soviet Union assembled at Moscow. Towards its end Khrushchev astounded the delegates by making a violent attack on Stalin's régime. He arraigned Stalin for promoting a cult of personality (an accusation that was later to be aimed at Mao Tse-tung) and for using terror to reinforce his dictatorship, which reduced the Communist Party to a pliant instrument of his personal rule.[1] The policy of de-Stalinization, thus launched, was enthusiastically endorsed and, as news of the secret speech filtered through, the whole country was thrown into a 'fever'.[2] Khrushchev's speech, which made such an enormous impact on the domestic affairs of Russia, was the climax of the proceedings. However, the congress was also a significant event in the development of the foreign policy of the Soviet Union.

According to Pethybridge '. . . the Twentieth Congress presented an abstract résumé of the main lines of Soviet foreign policy since Stalin. For the most part it did not launch a new series of changes, but rather altered the existing ideological line, which lagged behind the reality of political action. At the same time it provided a useful platform for explaining the deeper meaning of Soviet policy to the world: it attempted to impress the West (by the theory of peaceful co-existence), Eastern Europe (by the concept of different roads to socialism), and the uncommitted countries (by the theoretical rejection of violent revolution) that Stalinism had been abandoned.'[3]

'Peaceful co-existence' was the most significant concept and it is important to understand precisely what the Soviets meant by that term. It did not imply a rejection of the basic Marxist belief that capitalism was doomed. Khrushchev, no less than Stalin, perhaps more than Stalin, believed in the final victory of Communism. The question was how to facilitate that victory. The destructive power of thermonuclear weapons ruled out a war between the

Delegates at the Twentieth Congress of the CPSU listen to Khrushchev's new line.

USA and the Soviet Union: the danger of mutual destruction was too great. This did not prohibit the use of force in certain circumstances. Conventional weapons would be retained (though in August 1955 it was announced that the Soviet armed forces were to be reduced by 640,000 men).[4] The main struggle, however, would be economic. In the words of Deutscher, written just after the congress: 'Having broken the Western, or rather the American, monopoly of atomic and hydrogen weapons, they plan to use the time at their disposal for breaking another, equally decisive, monopoly the West has enjoyed so far – the monopoly of a high standard of living. They argue that it is up to the West to defend this, its advantage, with all its economic might; and that it is legitimate for the Soviet Union to challenge the West on this ground. Such is the meaning of "peaceful competition" in peaceful co-existence.'[5] There was, of course, no doubt about the outcome of the struggle. The prosperity of the West was bound to collapse in a disastrous slump. Thus the uncommitted would be convinced 'through their stomachs' of the merits of Communism. While this pre-determined economic conflict proceeded 'the broad purpose of Soviet diplomacy [was] . . . to preserve the international *status quo*.'[6]

Khrushchev considered that the *status quo* favoured the Soviet Union. He understood it to mean, inter alia, the continued existence of anti-colonial nationalist movements throughout the world. He anticipated that in Egypt, for example, Nasser would continue to resist Western attempts to preserve their influence and thus would open up the area to the Soviets. Unlike the Western nations, the Soviet Union was not burdened with a colonial past, although historically Russia had been an expansionist power. Anti-imperialism was a central tenet of Marxist–Leninist ideology and a recurrent theme in Soviet propaganda. Although the Russians exercised quasi-imperial power in Eastern Europe, peoples in Asia, Africa and the Middle East distrusted them less than they did the Western powers. They were less apprehensive of accepting economic aid from the Soviets, although it was found to increase Soviet influence.[7]

The Americans had helped to create this situation by seeing the hidden hand of the Kremlin in any demand for drastic economic and social change. Thus Dulles, mistaking Nasser for a Communist sympathizer, refused to finance the Aswan Dam project, in the summer of 1956, and so allowed the Soviets to step in and reinforce their influence in Egypt.[8] In fact Nasser was essentially an Arab nationalist and a fierce opponent of the Egyptian Communists. From the time of the Truman Doctrine, however, the United States had become the enemy of all revolutions. As Toynbee was to remark: '. . . America is today the leader of a world-wide anti-revolutionary movement in defence of vested interests.'[9] To the extent that nationalist revolutions were gaining ground, the US was constantly on the defensive and in danger of being out-manoeuvred by the Soviets. Paradoxically, the *status quo* was revolutionary. Thus, in proposing peaceful competition, Khrushchev believed that he was challenging the Western powers to a contest in which the odds were against them.

When nationalist revolutions threatened the Soviet bloc itself Khrushchev was less enthusiastic about them, although it was his attack on Stalin that had precipitated them. Inevitably, 'the uncovering of Stalin's mistakes sounded the death knell for his puppets, who in most cases were still in power in Eastern Europe. They had risen to the top on the crest of Stalin's infallibility; destruction of the myth involved their destruction also.'[10] Riots in Poland in June 1956, arising from economic grievances, soon created demands for political change. Throughout the summer and autumn of 1956 the country was in a state of crisis. The great mass of the people were obviously united in their hostility to the Stalinist police state which had subordinated Polish interests to the requirements of the Soviet Union. By their pressure, they succeeded in having Gomulka, a popular leader who had been imprisoned in 1951 for 'Titoism', returned to power. On 19 October he was elected First Secretary of the Communist Party and introduced a number of changes, notably a purge of the leading Stalinists in the party. The Soviet leaders acquiesced in the changes and seemed willing to see Poland controlled by an ex-Titoist, provided that his new policies did not threaten the safety of the Soviet Union.[11] This example of their greater flexibility was soon to be overshadowed by events in Hungary.

The Hungarians had the same cause for complaint as the Poles and were undoubtedly encouraged by the success of Gomulka. Owing to their pressure Gerö, who had earlier replaced the Stalinist Rakosi as First Secretary, agreed to the return of Imre Nagy as Premier on 24 October 1956. At the same time Gerö called on the Russian troops in Hungary to keep the situation under control. Instead of controlling it they inflamed it and during the last week of October fighting broke out in Budapest and other cities. Hundreds of political prisoners were released by armed students and workers and members of the secret police were attacked and killed. Nagy abolished the one-party system and indicated that Hungary would withdraw from the Warsaw Treaty. His announcement of the impending withdrawal was made a few hours before an Anglo–French ultimatum was delivered to Israel and Egypt; an ultimatum which was a pretext for armed intervention to reoccupy the Suez Canal which had been taken over by Nasser.

What followed has been well described by Singleton, whose account is more balanced than some other descriptions of the Hungarian uprising. 'It is likely,' he writes, 'that the preoccupation of the Western powers with the Suez crisis[12] helped to tip the scales in favour of Soviet intervention, although it is hardly likely that the Soviet Union would have tamely accepted the withdrawal from the Warsaw Treaty of one of its members, even if they had been prepared to acquiesce in the reappearance of the old political parties in Hungary. To many Communists the latter event was as shocking as the former, for it implied that the post-1945 revolution had failed. Nagy had struck a blow at the political cohesion of Eastern Europe as well as threatening the military security of the Soviet Union. It was apparent to Khrushchev that Nagy was no longer in control of the situation. Who knows what further concessions he might be forced to make? The American propaganda radio had urged the Hungarians to rise. Did this mean that American troops would move in to help the rebels? Many Hungarians expected American help. Who can blame Mr Khrushchev for jumping to the same conclusion? We shall probably never know exactly what happened in the Soviet Union at this time, and we can only suggest that the factors mentioned above may have weighed in the minds of the Soviet leaders, causing them to take their decision to intervene in great strength in Hungary shortly after they had announced the beginning of negotiations for a Soviet withdrawal in response to Nagy's earlier request.'[13]

The Red Army restored 'order' in Hungary at a dreadful price: the death of 30,000 Hungarians and 7,000 Russian troops. All the old fears about Soviet imperialism came flooding back and the Cold War became glacial. Hungary seemed to negate all the previous Soviet moves towards a *détente*. In the emotional aftermath of Budapest it was not easy to accept that the Soviet leaders, having used brute force to curb their satellites, might still favour accommodation with the West. 'As late as 17 November a significant Russian note still suggested the possible revision of the Warsaw Pact and a willingness to explore European divisions anew. The American government was obviously and sincerely affected by ... the brutal second Russian intervention in Hungary, but it preferred to demonstrate its sentiments in indignant rhetoric.'[14] The rhetoric failed to conceal how hollow the promises of liberation had been. As Ambrose has said: 'Liberation was a sham; it had always been a sham. All Hungary did was to expose it to the world. However deep Eisenhower's hatred of Communism, his fear of war was deeper. Even had this not been so, the armed forces of the United States were not capable of driving the Red Army out of Hungary, except through a nuclear holocaust that would have left all Hungary and most of Europe devastated. The Hungarians, and the other Eastern European peoples, learned that there would be no liberation, that they could not look forward to tying themselves to the West, that their traditional policy of playing East against West was finished. They would have to make the best deal they could with the Soviets. The Russian capture and execution of Nagy made the point brutally clear.'[15]

While war with the Soviets was unthinkable so, too, was negotiation. Eisenhower's own reluctance to deal with them was buttressed by the unremitting hostility of Dulles and by public opinion – especially the opinion of Americans of East European

The remains of a giant statue of Stalin, smashed during the Hungarian rising, Budapest, November 1956.

origin. However, as in the past, technological changes were to force the politicians and the people to think again. On 27 August 1957 the Soviet Union announced a successful test of an intercontinental ballistic missile (ICBM). According to a statement in the Soviet press: 'The results obtained show that it is possible to direct rockets into any part of the world.'[16] Soviet capacity in rocketry was dramatically demonstrated when they directed one of their rockets beyond this world. On 4 October the first earth satellite, *Sputnik I*, was launched. In the opinion of Horowitz: 'The main, irreducible meaning of the Sputnik . . . was the fact, from which there could no longer be any retreat, that the Soviet Union was a viable, competing social system, with an advanced technological base. Recognition of this reality caused a weakening of American confidence, and initiated the first steps of an agonizing reappraisal of the assumptions and the direction of American policies.'[17]

Agonizing reappraisal was to come later: the immediate result of the loss of confidence was to close ranks even tighter against the Communists. One of the first post-Sputnik American actions was to reject a Soviet offer – made on 10 December – to consider a ban on the stationing of nuclear weapons in Czechoslovakia, Poland, East Germany and West Germany. Noting that it had been the first time the Russians had been prepared to offer concessions in Czechoslovakia and Poland, Healey, the future Minister of Defence in Wilson's Labour Government, considered that the proposal might 'mark a turning point in Soviet diplomacy'.[18] Dulles ignored it and offered nuclear missiles to America's European allies. After initial dissent the NATO powers agreed to have intermediate range ballistic missiles (IRBMs) on their territory. Even so, on 9 January 1958, the Russians made another proposal to have summit talks on bomb tests, a nuclear-free zone in Central Europe and negotiations between the GDR and the Federal Republic of Germany. When that was also rejected they repeated their requests for top-level talks on 26 January. At the beginning of February a Republican editor in the US commented: 'As I see it we have the choice of negotiating with Russia or going to war . . . I am against the Dulles policies because they have proved sterile and unworkable. When Mr Dulles thought we held all the cards he was a "bluff and bluster" man. But nobody, including our Allies and Russia, was bluffed worth a damn . . . Mr Dulles has become a liability to peace.'[19]

A further Soviet note, on 1 March, called for a Foreign Ministers' meeting to arrange a summit conference. On 6 March Khrushchev offered to go to the United States and sent another note proposing negotiations. Having had no positive response to any of their proposals, the Soviets announced, on 31 March, that they were halting nuclear tests unilaterally.

'In a great address in the Senate on June 20, Fulbright contrasted the stubborn and rigid prosecution of the Cold War by Dulles with the realistic flexibility of Soviet policy and with the world's crying need for peace. We seemed to operate on the theory that serious negotiation could take place only if we were safely ahead in the arms race but would we "ever feel ourselves sufficiently ahead to negotiate?" Our leaders knew "that the world skirts the brink of disaster", indeed some had boasted of carrying it to that point. Administratively we were "organized to brand Soviet proposals within the hour", but not "to explore the feasibility of new proposals or to analyze old proposals in the light of the power orientation of recent years which may give them new meaning". The terrible alternative before us required "a vigorous unrelenting search for alternatives to destruction", regardless of who originated or proposed them".'[20]

Senator Fulbright pointed out: 'that Russian policy is not only what happened in Hungary. If it were only a question of military oppression, we would have . . . a much more easily defeated adversary. But Russian policy is also the military withdrawal from Finland; it is the Soviet signature of the Austrian Peace Treaty and subsequent military withdrawal from that country; it is also Russian acquiescence in the recent modification in Polish Communism; it is political support of the non-Communist nationalist movements in Asia and Africa and economic aid to the countries of these regions. It is, most of all, an almost continuous propaganda refrain calling for action to reduce the danger of nuclear warfare, coupled with proposals for a great variety of approaches to this fundamental international problem.'[21]

While Eisenhower and Dulles were being criticized for being too rigid, Khrushchev was under fire for being too conciliatory. Hard liners in the Kremlin and some of the Chinese leaders were very critical, for example, of his handling of a crisis in the Middle East in the summer of 1958. It was precipitated by the overthrow in

Iraq of the pro-Western Nuri es-Said.[22] At the invitation of President Chamoun of the Lebanon, a pro-Westerner himself who feared the spread of the Iraqi revolution, US marines landed in the Lebanon on 15 July. King Hussein, in a similar position, sought support from Britain and on 17 July British parachute troops arrived in Jordan. The objective in both places was, according to the *New York Times* correspondent, 'to restore Western prestige generally in the Middle East and to stabilize the friendly oil-producing governments in Saudi Arabia and the Persian Gulf region.'[23] Ambrose contends that the Russians were well aware of that objective: 'The Soviet ruler knew that Eisenhower acted to protect Western oil holdings and he knew how vital those holdings were to the West. As long as Eisenhower was willing to hold down the scope of the intervention, Khrushchev would not interfere.'[24] In fact on 19 July Khrushchev called for a meeting of the heads of governments of the USSR, the USA, Britain, France and India. On 22 July he accepted Eisenhower's suggestion that the meeting should take place within the framework of the United Nations Security Council. The meeting, however, did not materialize.

Between 31 July and 3 August Khrushchev visited Peking for talks with the Chinese leaders. After his return to Moscow, on 5 August, he withdrew his support for the summit meeting on the grounds that the Security Council was dominated (as indeed it was) by the USA and its allies. Naturally this about face was believed to be a direct result of his discussions in Peking. It would be wrong, however, to imagine that the Chinese had taken command of Soviet policy. In Deutscher's estimation: 'Mao certainly did not simply dictate policy to Khrushchev. He had to give as much as he took. While Khrushchev called off the planned summit meeting over the Middle East, Mao acknowledged publicly the merits of summit diplomacy in general and recognized in advance that Khrushchev would be acting correctly if he sought another summit meeting on some future occasion.'[25]

By his actions, however, Mao was soon to show that he favoured confrontation rather than negotiation. On 23 August the Chinese Communists began an almost daily bombardment of Quemoy. Dulles warned, on 4 September, that US forces would be used to protect the island and by the middle of the month a formidable air and naval force had been assembled in the Western

Pacific. Mao evidently hoped that the Russians would use their ICBMs as a threat to force the Americans to renounce their support of Chiang Kai-shek and allow the Communists to liberate Quemoy and later Formosa. Khrushchev, however, acted with caution, determined not to be dragged into a nuclear conflict with the United States. The Chinese later charged him with delaying his promises of support until they were too late. Lacking firm Soviet backing they suspended their bombardment of Quemoy on 6 October.[26]

While he felt able to proceed slowly and deliberately in the Quemoy crisis, Khrushchev was under great pressure to take a tough line with the West on the question of Germany. Western Germany was firmly committed to the Western camp. In May 1955 the Federal Republic had been accepted as a member of the NATO alliance. On the other hand, the Western powers refused even to give diplomatic recognition to the German Democratic Republic in East Germany. The GDR had, however, become a member of the Warsaw Pact, a military alliance of the Communist bloc which had been set up shortly after West Germany joined NATO. Thus by late 1958 two hostile states, both belonging to powerful armed alliances, confronted each other in Germany. Catastrophe was a permanent possibility. It became imminent when, on 10 November, Khrushchev announced his intention of handing over control of Berlin to the GDR, with whom the Western powers would be obliged to negotiate their rights of access to the city. The question arises why, having worked to avoid confrontation over Quemoy, he created a crisis over the more precarious issue of Berlin.

Fleming, commenting on the reasons for the crisis, writes: 'One was the almost unbearable offense which West Berlin was to the Communist East. It was a great glittering outpost of capitalism, luxurious by comparison, prosperous, bustling. The United States had poured $600 million into West Berlin . . . The economic comparison was damaging enough, but the comparison between the individual liberties in West Berlin and the regimented, tight police controls around it was still worse . . . Since 1949, 3,000,000 people had gone through the Berlin escape hatch and the population was declining . . . West Berlin also contained the greatest combination of espionage agencies ever assembled in one place. It was an almost unbelievable windfall to be able to pursue all the missions of modern "intelligence" agencies, including sabotage, 110 miles deep in "the enemy's" territory. The same advantage accrued to Western radio stations and all other propaganda arms.'[27]

The situation in Berlin, however, was of long standing and hardly explains why Khrushchev made his move late in 1958. One of the spurs to action may have been the rapid re-armament of Western Germany. Strengthened by the American provision of artillery capable of firing nuclear shells and planes that could carry nuclear bombs, Adenauer was reviving Soviet fears of German militarism. He was also on the point of forming, with France, Italy and the Benelux countries, a Common Market. Thus, both economically and militarily, West Germany was adding its weight to the Western bloc.[28]

It is clear that Khrushchev had several reasons for wishing to negotiate a settlement with the Western powers. Having failed in all his attempts to persuade them to negotiate, he may have decided to force them to the conference table by deliberately provoking a crisis. On 30 November he declared that he would take no action over Berlin if talks started within six months. Yet, during the visit of Macmillan, the British Premier, to Moscow in February 1959, Krushchev rejected a Western offer for a Foreign Minsters' conference. Macmillan warned of the unforeseen dangers that lay ahead, while in America Senator Lyndon Johnson observed that 'the countdown has begun'.[29] In March Khrushchev shifted his ground again and himself proposed a meeting of the Foreign Ministers. It was in this confused and perilous situation that Dulles departed from the international scene. On 16 April he resigned for reasons of health and died the following month.

Though it may sound harsh to say so, his death increased the chances of negotiating a settlement. Fleming's judgment is that: 'In a time when the world needed healing and unifying leadership, with a desperation which only the plunge toward nuclear annihilation could supply, Mr Dulles laboured mightily to divide the peoples sharply, belligerently and permanently.'[30] Macmillan visited Dulles in hospital a month before his resignation and recorded: 'He was *against* almost everything. He was strongly against the idea of a *Summit*; he did not much like the Foreign Ministers' Meeting. He thought we could "stick it out" in Berlin, and that the Russians would not dare to interfere with us . . . It was a splendid exhibition of courage and devotion. But I felt that his illness had made his mind more rigid and reverting to very fixed concepts. I felt also sorry for the President.'[31]

There were two sessions of the Foreign Ministers' Conference during the summer of 1959. No major decisions were taken but the conference did prepare the way for a meeting of the heads of government at the summit. Another step on the road to the summit was the remarkable visit of Khrushchev to the United States in September.[32] At the end of it he had several private meetings with Eisenhower at the President's Pennsylvania retreat of Camp David. In a statement issued after their talks, both men agreed 'that all outstanding international questions should be settled not by the application of force but by peaceful means through negotiation.'[33] Later, Eisenhower consulted his allies and Khrushchev accepted the West's invitation to a summit meeting at Paris on 16 May 1960.

The summit was doomed to failure even before the leaders arrived in Paris. On 5 May Khrushchev announced that four days previously an American plane had been shot down while flying over the Soviet Union. At once the US National Aeronautical and Space Administration claimed that one of its weather planes had inadvertently strayed across the border. Two days later Kruschchev revealed that the Russians were holding the pilot of the plane, an employee of the Central Intelligence Agency called Powers, and that it was in fact a spy plane. In their book about the CIA Wise and Ross point out: 'During the four years, starting in 1956, that the spy plane flew over Russia, it brought back invaluable data on Russian "airfields, aircraft, missiles, missile testing and training, special weapons storage, submarine production, atomic production and aircraft deployments". It flew so high (well over 80,000 feet) that the Russians were unable to shoot it down at first.'[34] The U-2 piloted by Powers had, according to Khrushchev, been shot down 1,200 miles inside Soviet territory and Powers had admitted that he was on a photo-reconnaissance mission. Khrushchev was 'patently angered by the affair'. Nevertheless, in 'two speeches at a meeting of the Supreme Soviet . . . he stressed that it was very likely that Eisenhower had known nothing of the plane's flight'.[35] Commenting on Khrushchev's statements, the *Manchester Guardian* noted 'their studied moderation, and his readiness to absolve Mr Eisenhower of any guilt or even knowledge of the actions he complains about'.[36]

Eisenhower responded by authorizing Herter, the new Secretary of State, to assert that the United States had the right to spy on the Soviet Union. On 11 May he assumed personal responsibility for the flights and did not indicate then that he was going to stop them. In fact he cancelled the flights on the following day but did not make his decision public; he did not even inform his old friend Macmillan. Khrushchev, in his own estimation 'an incorrigible optimist',[37] nevertheless went to Paris. However, he told de Gaulle, the Conference President, that he could not take part until the U-2 affair had been settled. He insisted that the US government should not only cancel the flights but also apologize for them and punish those responsible. Eisenhower then announced that further U-2 flights had been cancelled, 'but to Western suggestions that this should satisfy Moscow Khrushchev replied, "That's a lackey's way. When a gentleman slaps a lackey's face and then gives him a sixpence, the lackey at once says thank you . . . But we know who we are and whom we represent." '[38] Deutscher has remarked that: 'If Khrushchev had contented himself with the mere announcement of the suspension, his position in Moscow and within the Soviet bloc might have been gravely weakened.'[39]

De Gaulle suggested a recess and on the morning of 17 May Khrushchev went with Malinovsky, the Soviet Defence Minister, to inspect the 1914–18 battlefields on the Marne. 'A sudden invitation to attend a summit meeting was sent after the Soviet Premier. According to eye-witnesses, his face lit up when he saw the document, and he at once turned back to Paris.' At the same time, Presidential Press Secretary Hagerty issued a statement asserting that Soviet participation at the three o'clock meeting would be taken as a withdrawal of Khrushchev's conditions. Khrushchev was given a copy of this statement, which had been issued without clearing it with either the British or the French, 'and at this point the conference expired'.[40] On the following day Khrushchev made a violent attack on Eisenhower at a press conference. The intemperance of his language led most of the Western press to shift the blame for the collapse of the summit from the American President to the ranting Russian leader.

Such was the tragi-comic ending of a meeting which had taken so long to prepare and had aroused so many hopes. In one country its collapse was positively welcomed. A month before the conference convened the Chinese party journal *Red Flag* published the first of a series of articles called 'Long Live Leninism'. In effect it attacked Khrushchev's vision of co-existence which had led him on to the summit: 'It rejected the view that a nuclear war would destroy civilization, and declared that "on the ruins of destroyed imperialism the victorious peoples will create with tremendous speed a civilization a thousand times higher than the capitalist system, and will build their bright future".'[41]

Red Flag had brought into the open a controversy between the Russians and the Chinese over foreign policy which had been developing since 1956.

Ten

THE COLD WAR TRANSFORMED

The Sino–Soviet split has prompted an examination of the relations between China and Russia which is extremely important for students of the Cold War. In particular it gives a fresh perspective to the foreign policy of the Soviet leadership – for example, to the attitude of Stalin.

Stalin's policy towards China contradicts yet again the assumption that his main objective was the world-wide extension of Communism. Throughout the period of the civil war, when the Chinese Communists were struggling to survive against Chiang Kai-shek, Stalin hardly raised a finger to help them. Indeed he maintained cordial relations with the Kuomintang government. That policy did not change even after 1945, by which time Mao Tse-tung's forces had greatly extended their influence and were seriously contending for the control of the whole of China. In 1945 Stalin negotiated with Chiang for the recognition of Russian interests in Manchuria which the Tsar Nicholas II had been forced to renounce after the Russo–Japanese war of 1904–5. He later described his attitude to a Yugoslav delegation that visited Moscow in 1948: '... after the war we invited the Chinese comrades to come to Moscow and we discussed the situation in China. We told them bluntly that we considered the development of the uprising in China had no prospects, that the Chinese comrades should seek a *modus vivendi* with Chiang Kai-shek, and that they should join the Chiang Kai-shek government and dissolve their army.'[1]

Ignoring that advice, Mao continued the struggle and won a series of impressive victories against the armies of Chiang. Yet, as Doak Barnett points out: 'The Russians continued to maintain diplomatic relations with the Nationalists during this period ... and even though the Communist victory in the Chinese Civil War was clearly imminent, they negotiated with the Nationalists throughout 1949 to secure special Soviet economic rights in Sinkiang. Stalin was apparently still determined to guarantee Russian, as distinct from Communist, interests in China, and this ambition, which he continued to press even after 1949, had a significant influence on Sino–Soviet relations throughout the period of Stalin's rule.'[2] In the words of Deutscher: 'Afraid once again of "complications" – of massive American interference in Far Eastern areas adjacent to Soviet frontiers – Stalin was still – in 1948! – trying to recapture the Chinese *status quo* of 1928.'[3]

Mao's final victory convinced Stalin that he had to come to terms with a new situation. Thus in February 1950 the Chinese and Soviet governments signed a treaty of friendship, alliance and mutual assistance. Mao's signature confirmed his previously expressed view: 'Internationally, we belong to the anti-imperialist front, headed by the USSR . . . we can only look for genuine and friendly aid from that front and not from the imperialist front.'[4] The aid included long-term credits, amounting to $300 million, to allow China to obtain industrial, mining and railway equipment from the Soviet Union. At this stage Russian aid was critically important to the Chinese, enabling them to lay the foundations for their remarkable industrial expansion. As Deutscher put it: '. . . thanks to Soviet aid, the new China was not as isolated in the world as Bolshevik Russia had been in the years after 1917 . . . China was not at the outset reduced to her own desperately inadequate resources. Soviet engineering and scientific-managerial advice and Soviet training of Chinese specialists and workers eased the start of China's industrialization . . . Consequently, China did not have to pay the high price for pioneering in socialism that Russia had paid . . .'[5]

However, the Chinese themselves provided for the great bulk of their capital investment. 'In cash terms,' says Wilson, 'Russian aid financed only about two percent of the Chinese investment programme in the 1950s, and China received only about one eighth of Russia's total aid outflow (less than Poland or East Germany received, and only marginally more than tiny Mongolia). Subsequently Peking dispensed to other Afro–Asian governments more than she had received from the Soviet Union. Russian help was not charity, since the goods were mostly on credit and had ultimately to be paid for by the delivery of Chinese goods to Russia . . .'[6]

A significant part of the Chinese debt to the Soviet Union was incurred at the time of the Korean War. When China became involved the Russians provided military aid worth $2,000 million,[7] all of which was eventually paid for by the Chinese. Politically the effect of the war was to drive China and the Soviet Union closer together. In America, Mao was considered to be a particularly nasty Soviet puppet. On 18 May 1951, Dean Rusk, then Assistant Secretary of State for Far Eastern Affairs, declared: 'The Peiping[8] régime may be a colonial Russian government – a Slavic Manchukuo on a larger scale. It is not the Government of China. It does not pass the first test. It is not Chinese. It is not entitled to speak for China . . . The National Government of the Republic of China . . . more authentically represents the views of the great body of the people of China.' That statement reveals something of Americans' attitude to China:[9] it illustrates how difficult it was to accept the reality of a Communist government. Since it was unacceptable it had to be explained away – hence Rusk's fictional version of Sino–Soviet relations.

Through joint-stock companies the Russians did have some economic influence in China, but Mao was no puppet. The Chinese had made their own revolution, latterly against the advice of their Russian comrades. In terms of its population and its potential China was clearly a formidable power. Only the ignorant could imagine it was a Soviet satellite. Stalin, it is true, may have had some difficulty in admitting just how independent the Chinese were, though even he did not try to demand the compliance from Mao that he expected from Ulbricht in East Germany or Gottwald in Czechoslovakia. Stalin's successors reduced such Soviet influence as did exist in China. At the end of Khrushchev's visit in October 1954 it was announced that all Soviet troops would be withdrawn from Port Arthur. The Russians also agreed to hand over all their shares in Sino–Soviet joint-stock companies, their value to be refunded in goods over a number of years.[10] In May 1955 they promised to provide aid to China for the peaceful development of nuclear power.[11] A Soviet spokesman later claimed that there had been a significant improvement in their relations after the death of Stalin. 'This co-operation,' he said, 'reached its highest point after 1953 when, on the initiative of the Central Committee of the CPSU and of Comrade Khrushchev himself, all elements of inequality were removed in our relations – such elements having arisen from the Stalin "personality cult".'[12]

Ironically, it was Khrushchev's attack on Stalin that marked the starting point of the conflict between China and the Soviet Union. In his speech to the Twentieth Party Congress he expounded two theories that were to make him, in Chinese eyes, a traitor to the cause of international Communism. First, he denied that war was an inevitable concomitant of capitalism. Recognizing that that was one of the principles of Marxism–Leninism he had to justify his rejection of it. 'This precept,' he argued, 'was evolved at a time when imperialism was an all-embracing world system, and the social and political forces which did not want war were weak, poorly organized, and thus unable to compel the imperialists to renounce war . . . At the present time, however, the situation has radically changed. Now there is a world camp of Socialism which has become a mighty force . . . As long as capitalism survives in the world, the reactionary forces representing the interests of the capitalist monopolies will continue their drive towards military gambles . . . But war is not fatalistically inevitable.'[13] Secondly, Khrushchev accepted the possibility that the transition from capitalism to socialism could be made by peaceful means.

At a secret session of the congress, Khrushchev made a second speech in which he denounced Stalin, his former boss and the great leader and teacher of the Communist world.[14] The congress caused a great stir in all Communist countries, not least in China. According to Wilson: 'Mao and his Chinese colleagues were astonished that the Soviet leadership should announce such far-reaching policy changes, affecting the whole international Communist movement, without consulting the other Communist Parties. Stalin was much more than a dictator of Russia: he had led the world Communist cause through three eventful decades, and such men as Mao surely deserved the courtesy of advance warning that the Russian Party was now to turn its back on Stalin's memory? The Chinese disagreed with much that Stalin did, and were among the major victims of his mistakes, but they also found much to quarrel with in the Khrushchev platform.'[15] The lack of consultation indicated that Khrushchev and his colleagues still considered the Soviet Union to be the paramount authority in the Communist world, which, in terms of industrial and military power, it was. At this point the Chinese were not prepared to challenge that authority and, despite their misgivings, endorsed the Soviet criticisms of Stalin.[16]

Within a few months the Communist world was, as we have

seen, shaken by the events in Poland and Hungary.[17] In the course of the crisis that developed in Eastern Europe, China emerged as a major force in the Communist bloc. Subsequently the Chinese were to claim that the Soviet leaders 'committed the error of great-power chauvinism . . . by moving up troops in an attempt to subdue the Polish comrades by armed force'. They were also to allege that: 'At the critical moment when the Hungarian counter-revolutionaries had occupied Budapest, it [the CPSU] intended for a time to adopt a policy of capitulation and to abandon socialist Hungary to counter-revolution . . .'[18] The implication is that only Chinese intervention prevented the Russians from making terrible blunders. Gelman comments: 'Although it is quite likely that the Chinese have greatly exaggerated their part in determining the course ultimately taken by the Soviet Union in both the Polish and Hungarian crises, the essential point is that Peking apparently did intervene in an attempt to influence decisions that hitherto had been accepted as Moscow's sole prerogative.'[19] Clearly the Chinese were beginning to feel that they had the right and the duty to play a leading role in the world Communist movement.

Their next major initiative came after the Soviets had launched their ICBMs and sent Sputnik into orbit round the earth. Those developments, which caused consternation in America, convinced the Chinese that there had been a significant shift in the balance of power in the world. In November 1957, at the Moscow conference of the world's ruling Communist parties, Mao declared: 'I am of the opinion that the international situation has now reached a new turning point. There are two winds in the world today: the East wind and the West wind . . . I think the characteristic of the situation today is the East wind prevailing over the West wind. That is to say, the socialist forces are overwhelmingly superior to the imperialist forces.'[20]

On the surface, there was no disagreement between Mao and Khrushchev. Both recognized that the Soviet bloc had recovered from the convulsions of 1956 and that the military balance had moved in its favour. The question was how best to use its new strength. In the following months and years it became evident that Mao favoured using it to force the capitalists to give way. Khrushchev, on the other hand, wanted to force the West to negotiate a *modus vivendi*. Mao, paradoxically echoing Dulles, would drive

Khrushchev with Mao in Peking before the Sino–Soviet split had become public.

the enemy to the brink of war, from which they would retreat in confusion. By contrast, Khrushchev was pressing the Western powers to sit round the conference table, where both sides would make concessions. Peking sought world revolution: Moscow hoped to preserve the *status quo*.

Behind the Chinese was the ghost of Trotsky waving the banner of permanent revolution. At Khrushchev's elbow was the shade of Stalin sounding the old refrain of 'Socialism in One Country'.[21] The last great debate in the Communist movement had taken place in 1927, when Trotsky and Stalin had argued their case before the Executive Committee of the Communist International. After that Stalin had virtually banned open discussion. His death and the division of opinion between the Russians and the Chinese created the conditions for a new debate. It was to be conducted in the special language of Marxism, two concepts of which require some explanation. The first is 'revisionism'. It was a term first used to describe the ideas of Bernstein, a German Social Democrat who argued, at the end of the nineteenth century, that Marx's theories should be revised in view of subsequent political and economic developments. Thus it is applied to theories that are felt to depart from the basic principles of Marxism. The second expression is 'dogmatism' (otherwise 'sectarianism'), which denotes extreme left-wing ideas and policies which ignore 'objective reality', that is the realities of the existing political situation.[22]

The declaration issued at the end of the Moscow conference in November 1957 recognized the dangers of both those deviations from the 'true' principles of Marxism–Leninism. It said: 'In condemning dogmatism, the Communist parties believe that the main danger at present is revisionism – in other words, right wing opportunism as a manifestation of bourgeois ideology paralyzing the revolutionary energy of the working class and demanding the preservation or restoration of capitalism. However, dogmatism and sectarianism can also be the main danger at different phases of the development in one party or another. It is for each Communist party to decide what danger threatens it more at a given time . . .'[23] The events of the next few years were to show that Khrushchev, according to the Chinese, was the arch-revisionist while, in the Russian estimation, Mao was a misguided dogmatist.

During the summer of 1958 a crisis developed in the Middle East.[24] Khrushchev tried to reduce the tension with a letter to Eisenhower in which he said: 'We believe at this momentous hour that it would be more reasonable not to bring the heated atmosphere to boiling point; it is sufficiently inflammable as it is.'[25] An editorial in the *Chinese People's Daily* took a very different view. 'Consequently,' it said, 'if the US–British aggressors refuse to withdraw from Lebanon and Jordan, and insist on expanding their aggression, then the only course left to the people of the world is to hit the aggressors on the head! . . . The only language they understand is that of force.'[26] A meeting between Mao and Khrushchev patched over their differences but the gap between them was evidently widening.

It widened further at the time of the Quemoy crisis.[27] The Chinese appreciated that the Americans might use their nuclear weapons if war ensued.[28] Mao hoped, however, that, by throwing the weight of their nuclear power behind the Chinese, the

Soviets might force the US to back down. But the Russians only belatedly showed that they were willing to stand by their comrades and their previous hesitation indicated to the Americans that they would not, in fact, risk a nuclear showdown. The Russians obviously felt that the Chinese were adventurers who were blind to the danger of a thermonuclear holocaust. To the Chinese, Khrushchev was a revisionist kow-towing to the imperialists.

Disputes over foreign policy were paralleled by disagreements about domestic issues: 1958 was the year of the Great Leap Forward and the communes.[29] 'The Chinese leaders,' says Dutt, '. . . hoped to telescope the time of several decades that were normally required for industrialization and economic development into three or four – at the maximum, five years. This they hoped to achieve by making the people work harder and by undertaking simultaneous development of industry and agriculture . . . The Great Leap and the People's Communes got into full swing by the fall of 1958. The fancied phenomenal success of the new policies and reports of fantastic increases in production – highly exaggerated as they later turned out – generated an atmosphere of over-weening confidence in Peking . . . The Chinese leaders believed that they had found the key to the solution of their problems and hoped to catch up with the advanced countries of the world in a short period.'[30] Indeed, in terms of political organization they considered themselves to be in the vanguard, ahead even of the Soviet Union. 'Chinese spokesmen exuberantly claimed that the communes, with their system of partial distribution according to need, contained "shoots" of Communism, signifying that the final attainment of Communism in China was no longer far off; that they represented an unprecedented achievement as well as a useful model for other countries. In these claims and the policies of the Great Leap as a whole, the CPSU saw a new and dangerous Chinese challenge to its leadership of the Communist world.'[31] A writer in *Pravda* later commented: 'But for the . . . decisions of Mao and his colleagues, the Chinese People's Republic could have successfully continued along its socialist course after 1957. Instead, ignoring the experience of the other socialist countries, Mao and his friends tried to replace the normal industrialization process by the creation of countless primitive artisan enterprises . . . and the creation of both urban and rural "communes" in which people were to live like soldiers . . . All warnings from the Chinese people's foreign friends were ignored.'[32]

By the end of 1958 the Russians considered China to be the maverick of the Communist world. It seems that there was some support for their view in China itself. At a meeting of the central committee of the Chinese Communist Party in December, a resolution was passed declaring that industrialization would take a very long time. It said also that the transition from socialism to Communism would take 'fifteen, twenty or more years'. The committee approved a proposal by Mao that he should resign as Chairman of the Republic, while remaining Chairman of the Party. 'It was widely suggested that he had been forced to resign because of the failure of the communes, the plan to double steel production, and Chinese policy on the offshore islands.'[33]

The demotion, if that is what it was, of Mao did not, however, prevent a worsening of Sino–Soviet relations. On 20 June 1959 the Soviets repudiated a secret agreement, made in October 1957, by which they were to provide scientific information and technical materials necessary for China to make its own nuclear weapons. This repudiation was intended, according to a later Chinese statement, 'as a gift for the Soviet leader to take to Eisenhower when visiting the USA in September'.[34] Khrushchev's visit was, as we have seen, part of his campaign for a summit meeting.[35] During it he reiterated the danger of nuclear war, appealed for peaceful co-existence and frequently praised Eisenhower. After returning to Moscow he maintained that the US President 'sincerely wants to liquidate the cold war and improve relations between our two great countries'. Such remarks grossly offended the Chinese who were to comment that 'no considerations of diplomatic protocol can explain away or excuse Khrushchev's tactless eulogy of Eisenhower and other imperialists'.[36]

Soviet enthusiasm for a *rapprochement* with the USA was contrasted with its rigid neutrality over border incidents involving India and China. After a clash at Longju, in August 1959, Tass, the Soviet News Agency, pointed out that the Soviet Union maintained friendly relations with both countries and declared that 'attempts to exploit the incidents . . . for the purpose of fanning the cold war . . . should be resolutely condemned'.[37] When a second incident occurred in October at Ladakh, the Soviet press 'adopted a completely neutral attitude towards the incident, printing the Indian and Chinese versions side by side without comment'.[38]

Summing up an eventful year, Gelman notes: 'As the Chinese saw it, Khrushchev's actions during 1959 had set virtually a new record of error and betrayal: he had rebuffed them on the question of atomic military assistance, sought to interfere in Chinese internal affairs, hobnobbed with the leaders of "US imperialism", betrayed them in the Sino–Indian conflict, intimated that they should renounce their claim to Taiwan,* and upbraided them publicly for their domestic and foreign policies. It is little wonder, therefore, that in April 1960 the CCP unleashed a massive propaganda assault aimed at the policies – and, implicitly, the authority – of the Soviet Communist Party.'[39] A series of articles in the Chinese press implied that the Russians were advancing rapidly on the road to revisionism. Their criticisms were ostensibly directed at the 'Yugoslav revisionists' but there was no doubt that they were, in fact, attacking the policies of Khrushchev and his colleagues. The Soviets responded by condemning 'dogmatism' without stating openly that they considered Mao to be the arch-dogmatist.[40]

In June 1960 representatives of both sides met at Bucharest in an attempt to resolve their differences. Khrushchev tried to defend his policy of seeking to negotiate with the West. 'The great Socialist camp,' he declared, 'which now numbers over 1,000,000,000 people, is growing and gaining in strength. The organization and political consciousness of the working-class have grown, and even in the capitalist countries it is actively fighting for peace ... One cannot mechanically repeat now on this question what Lenin said many decades ago on imperialism, and go on asserting that imperialist wars are inevitable until Socialism triumphs throughout the world ... One cannot ignore the ... changes in the correlation of forces in the world, and repeat what the great Lenin said in quite different historical conditions.' The principal Chinese delegate, however, affirmed that 'as long as imperialism exists there will always be a danger of aggressive war'. At the end of the conference a communiqué was issued which tried to reconcile the Russian and the Chinese attitudes. It was clear, however, that a genuine reconciliation had not been

* The island elsewhere named Formosa.

reached. Both parties did agree to convene a world Communist conference in Moscow.[41]

Within a month the Soviet government announced that in August 1960 it would withdraw all Soviet technicians working in China. 'This unilateral decision, which aroused greater resentment in China than any other action of the Soviet Government, with the possible exception of the repudiation of the agreement on nuclear weapons, struck a crushing blow at China's economy at a time when the country was suffering from a series of natural disasters described by Peking Radio as "without parallel in the past century", including drought, typhoons, floods, and plagues of locusts and other insects. According to later Chinese statements, 1,390 experts were withdrawn, 343 contracts concerning technical aid cancelled, and 257 projects of scientific and technical cooperation ended, with the result that many projects in progress had to be suspended and some factories and mines which were conducting trial production could not go into production according to schedule.'[42] Two Western observers were told subsequently: 'It was like taking the dishes out in the middle of a meal'.[43]

Despite this blow, the Chinese attended the conference of 81 Communist parties which opened at Moscow in November. Once again the two main disputants were unwilling to reveal to the capitalist world the extent of the divisions between them. Another compromise statement was produced. 'The signature of the conference declaration was accompanied by the customary public pledges of undying solidarity and mutual affection, but privately neither Moscow nor Peking regarded the compromise as anything but a temporary makeshift, nor did either intend to abandon the struggle.'[44] Within a few years it became completely open and increasingly bitter. There were numerous border incidents and in March 1969[45] armed clashes between Soviet and Chinese frontier guards caused considerable loss of life. These later developments followed logically from the positions that both sides had taken by 1960. It is now clear that by that date the Communist movement was divided on crucial questions of domestic and foreign policy. The Chinese felt that Soviet revisionists were betraying the revolution within the Soviet Union and were undermining world revolutionary forces by their treacherous policy of compromising with American imperialism. On the other hand, the Russians held that Mao and his clique were perverting the revolution in China and were promoting a personality cult surpassing the Stalinist aberration exposed by Khrushchev in 1956. Furthermore the Chinese were pursuing an irresponsible foreign policy which, ignoring the 'objective reality' of the situation, threatened to precipitate a Third World War.

The Sino–Soviet split helped to create a new situation in which the Cold War ceased to be the dominant issue. In the decade following 1960 the mutual antagonism of China and the Soviet Union became more intense than the antipathy between the Americans and the Russians. Barraclough has noted that one of the important developments of that period was 'the gradual subsidence of the ideological conflict between the Soviet Union and the United States and the indications that, confronted by a new constellation of forces, the two countries were seeking to find a basis for *rapprochement*'.[46] That basis was more attainable as a result of changes in Soviet society. Under Khrushchev conservative elements gained further ground and the revolutionary fervour of the early Bolshevik generation became a thing of the past. As in the West, the mass of the people were more interested, by the close of the sixth decade of the twentieth century, in enjoying the benefits of affluence than in prosecuting an ideological crusade. These were significant facts. They indicated – in conjunction with such developments as peaceful co-existence and thermonuclear stalemate – that the "cold war" which had been the mark of the transitional period, was drawing to a close.'[47]

One of the features of the new situation was the increasing importance of the Third World. In their attitudes to this group of underdeveloped and uncommitted countries the Chinese and the Russians once again diverged. As Lane points out: 'Soviet policy . . . was to secure friends among the "uncommitted" nations of the world, whatever their political complexion. If they were "uncommitted" they were not part of the capitalist bloc, and therefore weakened it. Soviet influence could also be used, it was argued, to keep societies moving from feudalism to capitalism on a progressive path. But the Chinese tended to support the revolutionary underdogs in the developing countries . . . they criticized the soft "reformist" line of the Russians in Iraq and Syria when they restrained the Communist parties of those countries.'[48] Deutscher's point on this issue can hardly have been missed by the Chinese.

He says: 'Khrushchev's policy in the Middle East has been almost a replica of Stalin's policy in China in 1925–7, when Stalin considered Chiang Kai-shek as his ally and urged the Chinese Communist Party to accept Chiang's leadership and submit to Kuomintang discipline.'[49]

'For underdeveloped China,' comments Lane, 'a greater commitment was demanded from the Soviet Union to fulfil the ideological goal of a Communist world over Russia's own desire for internal well being.'[50] The Chinese did not, however, expect their demand to be met. The typical Soviet attitude was well put by two American observers: 'It is difficult to believe that the ordinary Russian is any longer much concerned for the ideological well-being of Afro–Asia or Latin America – except in the vague sense that Americans assert that the world some day must share the American dream. The progress of proletarian revolution . . . has become increasingly an empty slogan, to be repeated at May Day festivals.'[51]

From Peking it seemed that Moscow and Washington were set on similar courses. By 1960 the Chinese leaders were conscious of '. . . the narrowing disparity between US and Soviet involvements, instruments and even intentions in the Third World.'[52] Both super-powers were, it seemed, preoccupied with their own self-interest, which, in both cases, demanded the world-wide containment of revolution. This view was oversimplified and ignored significant differences between the Russians and the Americans. It was realistic, however, in recognizing that 'the competition between the United States and the Soviet Union had subsided owing to the intrusion of China.'[53] The Cold War waged so unremittingly by Truman and Dulles was virtually finished. Khrushchev's Cuban adventure in 1962 was going against the tide and was followed, in 1963, by the Test-ban Treaty, which was more typical of the relaxation of tension between the Soviets and the USA.* Such relaxation did not, of course, signify an end to the American struggle against Communism. The cold, diplomatic war against Russia was soon to be overshadowed by a shooting war with the Communists in Vietnam. What we can see emerging after 1960 is a 'dual standard in ideology . . . with the United States permitting a *détente* with European Communism while remaining strict with its Asian varieties'.[54]

* For a further comment on the Cuban missile crisis see the Introduction.

REFERENCES

CHAPTER ONE

1. J. Reed, *Ten Days That Shook The World*, pp. 104–5.
2. For an introduction to Marx see R. Aron, *Main Currents in Sociological Thought*, Vol. 1 and T. B. Bottomore and M. Rubel (eds.), *Karl Marx, Selected Writings in Sociology and Social Philosophy*.
3. See D. Lane, *Politics and Society in the USSR*; L. G. Churward, *Contemporary Soviet Government*; M. Fainsod, *How Russia is Ruled*.
4. R. Rhodes James, *Churchill, A Study in Failure*, p. 106.
5. Ibid, p. 121.
6. Ibid, pp. 154–5.
7. N. Bukharin and E. Preobrazhensky, *The ABC of Communism*, p. 87.
8. Ibid, p. 67.
9. E. H. Carr, *The Bolshevik Revolution 1917–23*, Vol. 3, pp. 135–6.
10. R. H. Bruce Lockhart, *British Agent*, p. 108ff.
11. Ibid, p. 134.
12. G. F. Kennan, *Russia and the West Under Lenin and Stalin*, pp. 54–65.
13. Ibid, pp. 44–6.
14. See J. Bradley, *Allied Intervention in Russia*.
15. Quoted in R. H. Ullman, *Britain and the Russian Civil War*, p. 5.
16. M. Gilbert, 'The Intervention', article in *History of the 20th Century*, Vol. 3 Chap. 35, p. 974.
17. Kennan, op. cit., p. 108.
18. Ullman, op. cit., p. 7.
19. N. Gordon Levin Jr., *Woodrow Wilson and World Politics*, p. 87.
20. Lockhart, op. cit., p. 134.
21. Carr, op. cit., p. 121, n. 1.
22. M. Sayers and A. E. Kahn, *The Great Conspiracy*, p. 47.
23. *History of the Communist Party of the Soviet Union (Bolsheviks)*, p. 237.
24. Carr, op. cit., p. 123.
25. Bradley, op. cit., p. 214 says: 'Though the Allied decision to intervene in Russia involved no long-term consideration on the part of the Allies, the intervention had long-term repercussions in international relations. Even nowadays it is used as an argument against an East–West *détente*; it definitely influenced Stalin in 1939 when he spurned Western approaches and chose to ally himself with Germany.'
26. Carr, op. cit., p. 273.
27. Ibid., p. 304.
28. Kennan, op. cit., p. 206.
29. See I. Grey, *The First Fifty Years*, p. 258; W. LaFeber, *America, Russia and the Cold War*, p. 4.
30. Carr, op. cit., p. 380.
31. J. Harvey (ed.), *The Diplomatic Diaries of Oliver Harvey*, p. 179. For another view of Munich see M. Gilbert, *The Roots of Appeasement*.
32. G. Ingr, letter in *The Times*, 1 August 1970; J. Kosina, letter in *The Times*, 10 August 1970.
33. See Lord Boothby, letter in *The Times*, 11 June 1971.

34. A. O. Chubaryan, 'Anti-Soviet Conspiracy', article in *History of the 20th Century*, Vol. 4 Chap. 59, p. 1646.
35. Lord Butler, article in *The Times*, 18 May 1971.
36. Ibid.
37. I. Maisky, letter in *The Times*, 8 June 1971.
38. Grey, op. cit., p. 269 and p. 510. On the question of secret negotiations see also L. Schapiro, *The Communist Party of the Soviet Union*, p. 490.
39. *Keesings Contemporary Archives*, Vol. 3, p. 3698.
40. A. O. Chubaryan, 'The Soviet German Treaty of 1939', article in *History of the 20th Century*, Vol. 4 Chap. 60, p. 1659.
41. Keesings, op. cit., p. 3838.

CHAPTER TWO

1. For an excellent single-volume account of the Russian–German war see A. Werth, *Russia at War 1941–1945*.
2. W. S. Churchill, *The Second World War*, Vol. 3, p. 331.
3. D. Horowitz, *From Yalta to Vietnam*, p. 59.
4. W. S. Churchill, *The Second World War*, Vol. 4, p. 717.
5. J. P. Nettl, *The Soviet Achievement*, p. 157.
6. Ibid., p. 176.
7. S. Ambrose, *Rise to Globalism*, p. 46.
8. See J. K. Zawodny, *Deaths in the Forest*; Werth, op. cit., p. 584ff. and p. 598ff.
9. See Werth, op. cit., pp. 776–90.
10. I. Deutscher, *Stalin*, p. 510.
11. See W. S. Churchill, *The Second World War*, Vol. 6, pp. 197–8 and L. S. Stavrianos, *The Balkans since 1453*, pp. 818–20.
12. Deutscher, op. cit., p. 507fn.
13. Quoted in Diane Shaver Clemens, *Yalta*, p. 173.
14. For comprehensive accounts of the conference see Clemens, op. cit. and H. Feis, *Churchill Roosevelt Stalin*.
15. Horowitz, op. cit., p. 35.
16. Clemens, op. cit., p. 7.
17. D. Donnelly, *Struggle for the World*, p. 156.
18. Ibid, p. 158.
19. Quoted in Werth, op. cit., p. 870.
20. Clemens, op. cit., p. 177.
21. Ibid, p. 270.
22. Ambrose, op. cit., p. 111.
23. For Truman's attitude to the Russians see above p. 15.
24. Ambrose, op. cit., p. 112.
25. Ibid, p. 113.
26. Ibid, p. 114.
27. D. F. Fleming, *The Cold War And Its Origins 1917–1960*, Vol. 1, pp. 268–9.
28. Clemens, op. cit., p. 269.
29. J. V. Stalin, *Correspondence with Churchill, Attlee, Roosevelt and Truman*, Vol. 2, p. 220.

CHAPTER THREE

1. W. H. McNeill, *America, Britain and Russia*, p. 763.
2. See Levin, op. cit., p. 13ff.

3. Ambrose, op. cit., p. 17.
4. Ibid, pp. 17–21.
5. See above Chap. 1 n.3.
6. See above pp. 9–10.
7. Clemens, op. cit., p. 68.
8. Ibid, p. 94.
9. G. Kolko, *The Politics of War*, p. 619.
10. J. W. Fulbright, *Prospects for the West*, p. 6.
11. See Horowitz, op. cit., p. 37.
12. Ibid, p. 39 fn.
13. For a full account of Potsdam see H. Feis, *Between War and Peace*.
14. Deutscher, op. cit., p. 530.
15. A. H. Birse, *Memoirs of an Interpreter*, p. 207.
16. H. S. Truman, *Memoirs*, Vol. 1, p. 342.
17. Ambrose, op. cit., p. 126.
18. Ibid, p. 125.
19. Truman, op. cit., p. 341.
20. Quoted in Horowitz, op. cit., pp. 57–8.
21. W. S. Churchill, *The Second World War*, Vol. 6, p. 553.
22. Quoted in Gar Alperovitz, *Atomic Diplomacy: Hiroshima and Potsdam*, p. 189.
23. Fleming, op. cit., p. 306.
24. Alperovitz, op. cit., p. 237.
25. Ibid, p. 238.
26. Ibid, p. 242.
27. P. M. S. Blackett, *Military and Political Consequences of Atomic Energy*, p. 127.
28. Alperovitz, op. cit., p. 130.
29. Ibid, p. 202.
30. Ibid, p. 229.
31. Ambrose, op. cit., p. 127.
32. W. S. Churchill, *The Second World War*, Vol. 6, p. 554 and pp. 579–80.
33. E. Crankshaw (ed.), *Khrushchev Remembers*, p. 361.
34. Quoted in Fleming, op. cit., p. 329.
35. Truman, op. cit., p. 342.
36. See Mao Tse-tung, *Selected Works*, Vol. 4, pp. 97–101.
37. P. M. S. Blackett, *Atomic Weapons and East–West Relations*, p. 87.
38. Ambrose, op. cit., p. 128–9.
39. Quoted in Blackett, *Military and Political Consequences etc.* p. 74.
40. Fleming, op. cit., p. 308.
41. Ambrose, op. cit., p. 129.
42. See Fleming, op. cit., pp. 337–8.
43. For attempts to get agreement on the control of atomic energy in the crucial post-war period see Fleming, op. cit., pp. 363–415; Blackett, *Military and Political Consequences etc.* Chaps. IX, XI, XII, XIII, XIV; R. G. Hewlett and O. E. Anderson, *A History of the United States Atomic Energy Commission*, Vol. 1.
44. Fleming, op. cit., p. 339.
45. Ibid.
46. Quoted ibid.
47. Truman, op. cit., pp. 491–2.
48. Ibid, p. 493.
49. Fleming, op. cit., p. 340.
50. L. J. Halle, *The Cold War As History*, p. 39.
51. See *Keesings*, Vol. 6, pp. 7753–4.
52. Fleming, op. cit., p. 348.

53. Quoted in L. Fischer, *This is Our World*, p. 49.
54. Ambrose, op. cit., p. 131.
55. Horowitz, op. cit., p. 84.
56. Fleming, op. cit., p. 346. 'The impression made upon the British *New Statesman and Nation* was not that of a Machiavellian Power pursuing a calculated course of aggrandizement, but rather of a blundering and suspicious giant, throwing its weight around and hurting itself and everyone else.'
57. For the complete speech see *Keesings*, Vol. 6, pp. 7770–2.
58. I. Ehrenburg, *Post War Years 1945–54*, p. 41.
59. Quoted in Fleming, op. cit., p. 354.
60. Fleming, op. cit., p. 350.
61. Ibid, p. 351.
62. F. Williams, *A Prime Minister Remembers*, pp. 162–3.
63. Quoted in Fleming, op. cit., p. 355.
64. Ibid, p. 357.
65. *Keesings*, Vol. 6, p. 7793.

CHAPTER FOUR

1. Halle, op. cit., pp. 105–6.
2. Ibid, p. 106.
3. Horowitz, op. cit., p. 60.
4. Halle, op. cit., p. 106.
5. Ambrose, op. cit., p. 140.
6. Fleming, op. cit., Vol. 2, p. 1061.
7. See Horowitz, op. cit., p. 28 fn.
8. Blackett, *Atomic Weapons and East–West Relations*, p. 69.
9. Horowitz, op. cit., p. 29.
10. Halle, op. cit., p. 80.
11. See above Chap. 2, n.11.
12. W. Laqueur, *Europe Since Hitler*, p. 90.
13. Fleming, op. cit., Vol. 1, p. 182.
14. Stavrianos, op. cit., pp. 826–8.
15. Fleming, op. cit., Vol. 1, p. 182.
16. Howard K. Smith, *The State of Europe*, p. 232.
17. E. O'Ballance, *The Greek Civil War*, p. 122.
18. M. Djilas, *Conversations with Stalin*, p. 102.
19. Quoted Fleming, op. cit., Vol. 1, p. 423.
20. Ibid, p. 424.
21. Ibid, p. 433.
22. McNeill, op. cit., p. 609.
23. Horowitz, op. cit., p. 95.
24. They referred particularly to alleged Communists in the USA.
25. Horowitz, op. cit., p. 97.
26. Fleming, op. cit., Vol. 2, p. 1064.
27. See Smith, op. cit., p. 232: 'With or without the aid of the Communists, it is very likely that the civil war would have been resumed in Greece.'
28. Ambrose, op. cit., p. 142.
29. Smith, op. cit., p. 22.
30. Quoted Fischer, op. cit., p. 81. Britain had been giving financial and economic aid to Turkey.
31. For the text see W. LaFeber (ed.), *America in the Cold War*, pp. 49–55.

References

32. H. S. Truman, *Memoirs*, Vol. 2, p. 111.
33. LaFeber (ed.), op. cit., p. 53.
34. Ambrose, op. cit., p. 150.
35. Laqueur, op. cit., p. 87.
36. Donnelly, op. cit., p. 230.
37. Halle, op. cit., p. 113.
38. Ibid, p. 140.
39. Alperovitz, op. cit., p. 234.
40. Smith, op. cit., pp. 115–16.
41. See Fleming, op. cit., Vol. 1, p. 453.
42. Ibid, p. 450.
43. Quoted Ambrose, op. cit., p. 151.
44. Ibid, p. 152.
45. Ibid, p. 142.
46. Ibid, p. 151.
47. Ibid, p. 150.
48. *Keesings*, Vol. 6, p. 8493.
49. Fleming, op. cit., Vol. 1, p. 478. The first part of his remark might appear to be rather too sanguine.
50. Quoted Halle, op. cit., pp. 151–2.
51. *Keesings*, Vol. 6, p. 8659.
52. Ibid, p. 8684.
53. Truman, *Memoirs*, Vol. 2, p. 121.
54. Ibid, p. 126.
55. Ambrose, op cit., p. 156; Horowitz, op. cit., p. 72 fn. quotes Rostow: 'One fear was that if the Russians accepted it, the US Congress would not finance it.'
56. Ambrose, op. cit., p. 157; Horowitz, op. cit., p. 70; Smith, op. cit., pp. 94–5.
57. Quoted, Fleming, op. cit., Vol. 1, p. 479.
58. Quoted in F. Greene, *The Enemy*, p. 116.
59. Ibid, p. 117.
60. W. A. Williams, *The Tragedy of American Diplomacy*, pp. 14–15.
61. Ibid, p. 17.
62. See Horowitz, op. cit., p. 72.
63. Smith, op. cit., p. 87.

CHAPTER FIVE

1. Horrowitz, op. cit., p. 80.
2. R. W. Pethybridge, *A History of Postwar Russia*, p. 37.
3. Ibid, p. 38.
4. Keesings, Vol. 6, p. 8648.
5. Ibid, pp. 8847–8.
6. Ibid, p. 9042.
7. Ibid, p. 8928.
8. Ibid, p. 9154.
9. Halle, op. cit., p. 142.
10. Paul-Henri Spaak, *Why NATO?*, p. 11.
11. Smith, op. cit., pp. 282–3.
12. Ibid, p. 360.
13. Ibid, pp. 284–5.
14. F. B. Singleton, *Background to Eastern Europe*, p. 201.
15. Smith, op. cit., p. 267.

127

16. Ibid, pp. 358–9.
17. H. Seton-Watson, *The Pattern of Communist Revolution*, p. 250.
18. Ibid, p. 255.
19. Stavrianos, op. cit., p. 842.
20. Ibid, p. 839.
21. Nettl, op. cit., p. 180.
22. Smith, op. cit., p. 368.
23. Deutscher, op. cit., p. 569.
24. Fleming, op. cit., Vol. 1, p. 482; Djilas, op. cit., pp. 100–1.
25. Quoted in L. Jay Oliva (ed.), *Russia and the West from Peter to Khrushchev*, p. 243.
26. *Keesings*, Vol. 6, p. 8864.
27. Singleton, op. cit., p. 175.
28. Pethybridge, op. cit., p. 101.
29. Smith, op. cit., p. 340.
30. Nettl, op. cit., p. 182.
31. Smith, op. cit., p. 343. There were to be tears enough in 1968.
32. F. W. Neal, *US Foreign Policy and the Soviet Union*, p. 18; Smith, op. cit., pp. 343–7.
33. Nettl, op. cit., p. 182.
34. Horowitz, op. cit., p. 78.
35. On the Tito–Stalin rift see Fleming, op. cit., Vol. 1, pp. 510–14.
36. V. Dedijer, *Tito Speaks*, p. 234.
37. Singleton, op. cit., p. 186.
38. Ibid, p. 187.
39. For Tito's version of the break see Dedijer; see also Deutscher, op. cit., pp. 577–9.
40. Horowitz, op. cit., 79–80.

CHAPTER SIX

1. Djilas, op. cit., p. 90.
2. Ibid, pp. 90–1.
3. Ibid, p. 119.
4. Smith, op. cit., p. 107.
5. Ibid, pp. 103–5.
6. Ibid, p. 102.
7. Ibid. p. 107.
8. F. S. Northedge, *British Foreign Policy*, p. 73.
9. Smith, op. cit., p. 113.
10. Ambrose, op. cit., pp. 121–2.
11. Quoted in R. Steel, 'Did Anyone Start the Cold War?', article in the *New York Review of Books*, 2 September 1971, p. 27.
12. A. Werth, *France 1940–1955*, p. 308.
13. *Keesings*, Vol. 6, p. 8116.
14. Alperovitz, op. cit., p. 173.
15. Ambrose, op. cit., p. 144.
16. Ibid.
17. Ibid, p. 154.
18. Ibid, p. 155.
19. *Keesings*, Vol. 6, p. 9167.
20. See Ambrose, op. cit., pp. 170–1.
21. Ibid, p. 171.
22. H. W. Koch, 'The Two Germanies', article in *History of the 20th Century*, Vol. 6, Chap. 84, p. 2328.

23. Ibid.
24. *Keesings*, Vol. 6, 9338.
25. See P. Windsor, 'The Blockade of Berlin', in *History of the 20th Century*, Vol. 5 Chap. 77, pp. 2144–8.
26. Fischer, op. cit., p. 108.
27. Djilas, op. cit., p. 141.
28. Ambrose, op. cit., pp. 171–2.
29. Deutscher, op. cit., p. 574.
30. Fleming, op. cit., Vol. 1, p. 575.
31. Ambrose, op. cit., p. 174.
32. Ibid, p. 179.
33. See L. S. Kaplan (ed.), *NATO and the Policy of Containment*, pp. 18–22.
34. Ibid, pp. 23–7.
35. Quoted in Fleming, op. cit., Vol. 1, p. 537.
36. See Koch, op. cit., p. 2329.
37. Ibid, p. 2330.

CHAPTER SEVEN

1. See H. Higgins, *From Warlords to Red Star*, Chaps. 4 and 5.
2. Quoted in S. and R. Gelder, *Long March to Freedom*, p. 49.
3. Higgins, op. cit., pp. 77–8.
4. LaFeber (ed.), *America in the Cold War*, p. 73.
5. J. Major, 'McCarthy and the Communist Witch-Hunt', article in *History of the 20th Century*, Vol. 6 Chap. 82, p. 2279; Fleming, op. cit., Vol. 1, p. 532.
6. Horowitz, op. cit., p. 107.
7. LaFeber (ed.), op. cit., pp. 74–7.
8. See, however, the view of Ambrose, op. cit., p. 181: 'The Soviets now had two trumps, the bomb and the Red Army, to the West's one.'
9. Fleming, op. cit., Vol. 1, p. 528.
10. For details see ibid, pp. 530–1.
11. Ibid, p. 531.
12. Fleming, op. cit., Vol. 2, p. 632 quotes Lippmann's comment of the need for 'a Secretary of State who . . . does not have to appease his personal enemies'.
13. Horowitz, op. cit., p. 260.
14. See Fleming, op. cit., Vol. 2, p. 589ff.
15. Snow, *The Other Side of the River*, p. 714; Stone, *The Hidden History of the Korean War*, pp. 62–5.
16. Fleming, op. cit., Vol. 2, pp. 592–3; Horowitz, op. cit., p. 115.
17. Quoted in A. Guttmann (ed.), *Korea and the Theory of Limited War*, p. 67.
18. Deutscher, op. cit., p. 584: 'Having so recently and so scandalously misjudged the chances of the revolution in China, he was anxious to dispel the impression of political timidity he had given, and wanted to prove himself as daring a strategist of revolution as Mao.'
19. N. Sheehan *et al*, *The Pentagon Papers*, pp. 9–10.
20. Horowitz, op. cit., p. 120.
21. Ibid, p. 117.
22. Ibid, p. 120.
23. Stone, op. cit., Part I. *How The War Began*, pp. 1–66.
24. Ibid, p. 352.
25. Ibid, p. 44.
26. Horowitz, op. cit., p. 119; on the question of provocation and escalation in the Vietnam War see Sheehan *et al*. op. cit., p. 356 quoting memorandum attributed to

Assistant Secretary of Defense McNaughton: 'Actions . . . (3) they should be likely at some point to provoke a military . . . response [from N Vietnam], (4) the provoked response should be likely to provide good grounds for us to escalate if we wished . . .'

27. Salisbury, *The Coming War Between Russia and China*, p. 98.
28. Ibid, p. 103.
29. Crankshaw (ed.), *Khrushchev Remembers*, p. 368.
30. D. Rees, *Korea: The Limited War*, pp. 16–17.
31. Ibid, p. 36.
32. See, however, Adam B. Ulam, *Expansion and Co-existence*, pp. 518–19: 'The most widely accepted explanation of Soviet motivations is still the most logical one: looking at the situation from the Kremlin vantage point, there was no reason to suppose that there was any appreciable chance of an American intervention. It promised to be an easy tidying-up operation.'
33. Horowitz, op. cit., p. 121.
34. Stone, op. cit., p. 67.
35. Ibid, p. 77; Ambrose, op. cit., p. 197.
36. Stone, op. cit., p. 78; Ambrose, op. cit., p. 200.
37. Stone, op. cit., p. 70; Ambrose, op. cit., pp. 197–8.
38. Stone, op. cit., p. 71.
39. Ibid, pp. 99–100.
40. Ibid, pp. 124–38.
41. See Fleming, op. cit., Vol. 2, p. 1050.
42. Horowitz, op. cit., pp. 128–9.
43. Horowitz, op. cit., p. 129.
44. Stone, op. cit., pp. 89–92.
45. Ibid, p. 184.
46. F. Greene, *The Wall Has Two Sides*, p. 266.
47. Snow, op. cit., p. 714; A. S. Whiting, *China crosses the Yalu*, gives a comprehensive account of Chinese motives.
48. For a Chinese view see LaFeber (ed.), op. cit., pp. 80–2.
49. Quoted in Fleming, op. cit., Vol. 2, p. 631.
50. Horowitz, op. cit., p. 132.
51. See Ambrose, op. cit., pp. 211–13.
52. Ibid, p. 213.
53. Ibid, p. 210.
54. Quoted ibid, pp. 210–11.

CHAPTER EIGHT

1. Ambrose, op. cit., p. 217.
2. Fleming, op. cit., Vol. 2, p. 806.
3. Ibid, p. 812.
4. I. Deutscher, *Russia, China and the West 1953–1966* p. 12.
5. N. A. Graebner, *Cold War Diplomacy 1945–1960*, p. 166.
6. Ibid, p. 170.
7. Ibid.
8. On the destructive power of nuclear weapons see T. Stonier, *Nuclear Disaster*.
9. Horowitz, op. cit., p. 323.
10. Fleming, op. cit., Vol. 2, p. 1057.
11. Blackett, *Atomic Weapons etc.*, p. 82.
12. D. Lane, *Politics and Society in the USSR*, p. 114.
13. Deutscher, *Stalin*, p. 607.

14. Blackett, *Atomic Weapons etc.*, p. 82.
15. Deutscher, *Russia, China and the West*, p. 11.
16. See Churchill's comment on Molotov's visit to Chequers in May 1942, *The Second World War*, Vol. 4, p. 301: 'At night a revolver was laid out beside his dressing-gown and his dispatch case. It is always right, especially in time of war, to take precautions against danger, but every effort should be made to measure its reality.'
17. *Keesings*, Vol. 9, p. 12869.
18. Ambrose, op. cit., pp. 225–6.
19. See J. Lacouture, *Ho Chi Minh*, particularly Chaps. 8 and 9.
20. Sheehan *et al*, op. cit., p. 5.
21. Ibid, p. 10.
22. Ibid, p. 6.
23. Ibid, pp. 6–7.
24. Horowitz, op. cit., p. 147.
25. Sheehan *et al.*, op. cit., pp. 12–13.
26. Ibid, p. 13.
27. Ibid, p. 14.
28. Horowitz, op. cit., p. 148.
29. Sheehan *et al*, op. cit., p. 25.
30. *Keesings*, Vol. 10, p. 14118.
31. Ambrose, op. cit., p. 239.
32. Ibid, p. 240.
33. See Donnelly, op. cit., p. 389: '. . . the Soviet leaders had faced, at last, the inevitability of West German re-armament. In order to meet it, and concurrently with the Austrian Treaty preparations, they decided to reorganize the Communist defence pattern.'
34. Quoted in Pethybridge, op. cit., p. 146.
35. M. Frankland, *Khrushchev*, pp. 113–16; Crankshaw (ed.), op. cit., pp. 374–91.
36. Fleming, op. cit., Vol. 2, p. 751.
37. Crankshaw (ed.), op. cit., p. 392.
38. Ibid, p. 400.
39. Ambrose, op. cit., pp. 243–4.

CHAPTER NINE

1. For the text see Crankshaw (ed.), op. cit., pp. 559–618.
2. Frankland, op. cit., p. 126.
3. Pethybridge, op. cit., p. 190.
4. Horowitz, op. cit., p. 324.
5. Deutscher, *Russia, China and the West*, p. 68.
6. Ibid, p. 65.
7. See Fleming, op. cit., Vol. 2, pp. 1084–6.
8. Ambrose, op. cit., pp. 248–50.
9. A. Toynbee, *America and the World Revolution*, p. 16.
10. Pethybridge, op. cit., p. 191.
11. Singleton, op. cit., pp. 159–61.
12. On the crisis see H. Thomas, *The Suez Affair*.
13. Singleton, op. cit., pp. 146–7.
14. Quoted in Horowitz, op. cit., p. 291.
15. Ambrose, op. cit., p. 252.
16. Fleming, op. cit., Vol. 2, p. 863.
17. Horowitz, op. cit., p. 301.

18. Ibid, p. 309.
19. Ibid, p. 311.
20. Fleming, op. cit., Vol. 2, p. 941.
21. Ibid.
22. Fleming, op. cit., Vol. 2, pp. 921–2.
23. Horowitz, op. cit., p. 188.
24. Ambrose, op. cit., p. 255.
25. Deutscher, *Russia, China and the West*, p. 161.
26. *Keesings, The Sino–Soviet Dispute*, p. 16.
27. Fleming, op. cit., Vol. 2, p. 948.
28. Ambrose, op. cit., p. 259.
29. Fleming, op. cit., Vol. 2, p. 957.
30. Ibid, p. 956.
31. H. Macmillan, *Riding The Storm 1956–1959*, p. 644.
32. Frankland, op. cit., pp. 162–6.
33. *Keesings*, Vol. 12, p. 17082.
34. D. Wise and T. B. Ross, *The Invisible Government*, p. 122.
35. Frankland, op. cit., p. 168.
36. Horowitz, op. cit., p. 334.
37. Frankland, op. cit., p. 169.
38. Ibid.
39. Deutscher, *Russia, China and the West*, p. 201.
40. Horowitz, op. cit., p. 337.
41. *Keesings, The Sino–Soviet Dispute*, p. 26.

CHAPTER TEN

1. Dedijer, op. cit., p. 331. On this occasion Stalin, for once, admitted that he was not infallible: 'Now, in the case of China, we admit we were wrong. It has proved that the Chinese comrades and not the Soviet comrades were right.'
2. F. Schurmann and O. Schell (eds.), *Communist China*, p. 255.
3. I. Deutscher, *The Unfinished Revolution Russia 1917–1967*, p. 85.
4. Schurmann and Schell, op. cit., p. 255.
5. Deutscher, *The Unfinished Revolution*, p. 90.
6. Dick Wilson, *A Quarter of Mankind*, pp. 245–6.
7. *Keesings, The Sino–Soviet Dispute*, pp. 3–4.
8. Americans refused to call the city Peking (Northern Capital). Since Chiang Kai-shek was the rightful ruler, the capital was clearly Taipei, on the island of Formosa. See F. Greene, *A Curtain of Ignorance*, p. 5, n.2.
9. Horowitz, op. cit., p. 108.
10. *Keesings, The Sino–Soviet Dispute*, pp. 4–5.
11. Ibid, pp. 5–6.
12. Quoted in A. Werth, *Russia: Hopes and Fears*, p. 277.
13. *Keesings, The Sino–Soviet Dispute*, pp. 8–9.
14. See above, p. 103.
15. Wilson, op. cit., p. 247.
16. *Keesings, The Sino–Soviet Dispute*, p. 10.
17. See above, pp. 105–8.
18. Schurmann and Schell, op. cit., p. 265.
19. Ibid.
20. Wilson, op. cit., p. 248.
21. See H. Marcuse, *Soviet Marxism*, particularly Chap. 4.

22. See *Keesings, The Sino–Soviet Dispute*, pp. 13–14.
23. Ibid, p. 13.
24. See above, p. 111.
25. E. Crankshaw, *The New Cold War: Moscow v. Pekin*, p. 81.
26. Ibid. A curious echo here of Truman's comment on the Soviets.
27. See above, p. 112.
28. See D. Eisenhower, *Waging Peace*, p. 693.
29. For a recent account see E. L. Wheelwright and B. McFarlane, *The Chinese Road to Socialism*, pp. 43–53.
30. Schurmann and Schell, op. cit., pp. 156–7.
31. Ibid, p. 269.
32. Werth, *Russia: Hopes and Fears*, p. 272.
33. *Keesings, The Sino–Soviet Dispute*, p. 17.
34. Ibid, p. 19.
35. See above, p. 115.
36. *Keesings, The Sino–Soviet Dispute*, p. 20.
37. Ibid, pp. 19–20.
38. Ibid, pp. 21–22.
39. Schurmann and Schell, op. cit., p. 272.
40. *Keesings, The Sino–Soviet Dispute*, pp. 24–7.
41. Ibid, pp. 27–9.
42. Ibid, p. 29.
43. Wheelwright and McFarlane, op. cit., p. 53.
44. Schurmann and Schell, op. cit., pp. 275–6.
45. *Keesings, The Sino–Soviet Dispute*, pp. 116–19.
46. G. Barraclough, *An Introduction to Contemporary History*, pp. 228–9.
47. Ibid, p. 228.
48. Lane, op. cit., pp. 119–20.
49. I. Deutscher, *The Great Contest: Russia and the West*, p. 55.
50. Lane, op. cit., p. 121.
51. E. Stillman and W. Pfaff, *The New Politics: America and the End of the Postwar World*, p. 86.
52. R. E. Osgood *et al, America And The World, From the Truman Doctrine to Vietnam*, p. 348.
53. Ibid, p. 355.
54. Ibid, p. 407.

BIBLIOGRAPHY

Alperovitz, G., *Atomic Diplomacy: Hiroshima and Potsdam* (Secker & Warburg, 1965)

Ambrose, S. E., *Rise to Globalism* (Allen Lane, 1971)

Aron, R., *Main Currents in Sociological Thought*, Vol. 1 (Weidenfeld & Nicolson, 1965)

Barraclough, G., *An Introduction to Contemporary History* (Penguin, 1967)

Birse, A. H., *Memoirs of an Interpreter* (Michael Joseph, 1967)

Blackett, P. M. S., *Military and Political Consequences of Atomic Weapons* (Turnstile Press, 1948)
Atomic Weapons and East–West Relations (Cambridge University Press, 1956)
Studies of War (Oliver & Boyd, 1962)

Blumenfeld, H. *et al*, *Fifty Years of Soviet Power* (Monthly Review Press, 1967)

Bottomore, T. B. and Rubel, M. (eds.), *Karl Marx, Selected Writings in Sociology and Social Philosophy* (Penguin, 1963)

Bradley, J., *Allied Intervention in Russia* (Weidenfeld & Nicolson, 1968)

Bukharin, N. and Preobrazhensky, E., *The ABC of Communism* (Penguin, 1969)

Calvocoressi, P., *World Politics Since 1945* (Longmans, 1968)

Carr, E. H., *The Bolshevik Revolution 1917–1923*, Vol. 1 (Penguin, 1966)
The Bolshevik Revolution 1917–1923, Vol. 3 (Penguin, 1966)
The Interregnum 1923–1924 (Penguin, 1969)
Socialism in One Country, Vol. 2 (Penguin, 1970)

Chubaryan, A. O., 'Anti-Soviet Conspiracy', *History of the 20th Century*, Vol. 4 Chap. 59.
'The Soviet–German Treaty of 1939', *History of the 20th Century*, Vol. 4 Chap. 60

Churchill, W. S., *The Second World War*, Vol. 3 (Cassell, 1950)
The Second World War, Vol. 4 (Cassell, 1951)
The Second World War, Vol. 6 (Cassell, 1954)

Churchward, L. G., *Contemporary Soviet Government* (Routledge & Kegan Paul, 1968)

Clemens, D. S., *Yalta* (Oxford University Press, 1970)

Communist Party of the Soviet Union, History (Foreign Languages Publishing House, Moscow, 1939)

Crankshaw, E., *The New Cold War: Moscow v. Pekin* (Penguin, 1963)

Crankshaw, E. (ed.), *Khrushchev Remembers* (André Deutsch, 1971)

Dedijer, V., *Tito Speaks* (Weidenfeld & Nicolson, 1953)

Deutscher, I., *Stalin* (Oxford University Press, 1949.) (Revised and enlarged

edition, Penguin, 1966)
  The Great Contest: Russia and the West (OUP, 1960)
  The Unfinished Revolution Russia 1917–1967 (OUP 1967)
  Russia, China and the West 1953–1966 (Penguin, 1970)
Djilas, M., *Conversations with Stalin* (Penguin, 1963)
Donnelly, D., *Struggle For The World* (Collins, 1965)

Edwardes, M., *Asia in the Balance* (Penguin, 1962)
Ehrenburg, I., *Post War Years 1945–1954* (MacGibbon & Kee, 1966)
Eisenhower, D. D., *Mandate for Change* (Heinemann, 1963)
  Waging Peace (Heinemann, 1966)

Fainsod, M., *How Russia is Ruled* (Harvard University Press, 1967)
Feis, H., *Churchill Roosevelt Stalin* (Oxford UP, 1957)
  Between War and Peace (Oxford UP, 1960)
Fenno, R. F. (ed.), *The Yalta Conference* (D. C. Heath & Co., 1955)
Fischer, L., *This is Our World* (Jonathan Cape, 1956)
Fleming, D. F., *The Cold War And Its Origins*, 2 Vols (Allen & Unwin, 1961)
Frankland, M., *Khrushchev* (Penguin, 1966)
Fulbright, J. W., *Prospects for the West* (Harvard UP, 1963)

Garthoff, R. L., *Soviet Military Policy* (Faber & Faber, 1966)
Gelder, S. and R., *Long March to Freedom* (Hutchinson, 1962)
Gilbert, M., *The Roots of Appeasement* (Weidenfeld & Nicolson, 1966)
  'The Intervention', *History of the 20th Century*, Vol. 3, Ch. 35.
Goldman, E., *The Crucial Decade 1945–55* (Knopf, 1956)
Graebner, N. A., *Cold War Diplomacy 1945–1960* (Van Nostrand, 1962)
Greene, F., *A. Curtain of Ignorance* (Jonathan Cape, 1965)
  The Wall Has Two Sides (Jonathan Cape, 1964)
  The Enemy (Jonathan Cape, 1970)
Grey, I., *The First Fifty Years* (Hodder & Stoughton, 1967)
Guttmann, A., *Korea and the Theory of Limited War* (D. C. Heath & Co., 1967)

Halle, L. J., *The Cold War As History* (Chatto & Windus, 1967)
Harvey, J. (ed.), *The Diplomatic Diaries of Oliver Harvey 1937–1940* (Collins, 1970)
Hewlett, R. G. and O. E. Anderson, *A History of the United States Atomic Energy Commission* Vol. 1, *The New World 1939–1946* (University Park, 1962)
Higgins, H., *From Warlords to Red Star* (Faber & Faber, 1968)
Horowitz, D., *From Yalta to Vietnam* (Penguin, 1967)
Hull, C., *Memoirs*, 2 Vols (Hodder & Stoughton, 1948)

James, R. R., *Churchill, A Study in Failure* (Weidenfeld & Nicolson, 1970)

Kaplan, L. S. (ed.), *NATO and the Policy of Containment* (D. C. Heath & Co., 1968)
Keesings, *Contemporary Archives*
  The Sino–Soviet Dispute, 1970
  South Vietnam, A Political History 1954–1970 (Scribner's, 1970)
Kennan, G. F., *Russia and the West Under Lenin and Stalin* (Mentor, 1960)
Koch, H. W., 'The Two Germanies', *History of the 20th Century*, Vol. 6, Ch. 84.
Kogan, N., *A Political History of Postwar Italy* (Pall Mall Press, 1966)
Kolko, G., *The Politics of War* (Weidenfeld & Nicolson, 1969)
Krivitsky, W. G., *I Was Stalin's Agent* (Hamish Hamilton, 1939)

Lacouture, J., *Ho Chi Minh* (Penguin, 1969)
LaFeber, W., *America, Russia and the Cold War* (Wiley & Sons, 1967)
LaFeber, W. (ed.), *America in the Cold War* (Wiley & Sons, 1969)
Lane, D., *Politics and Society in the USSR* (Weidenfeld & Nicolson, 1970)
Laqueur, W., *Europe Since Hitler* (Weidenfeld & Nicolson, 1970)
Latham, E. (ed.), *The Meaning of McCarthyism* (D. C. Heath & Co., 1965)
Levin, N. G., *Woodrow Wilson and World Politics* (Oxford UP, 1968)
Lider, J., *West Germany in NATO* (Warsaw Press Agency, 1965)
Lippmann, W., *The Communist World and Ours* (Hamish Hamilton, 1959)
Lockhart, R. B., *British Agent* (Four Square Books, 1961)
Luard, E. (ed.), *The Cold War A Reappraisal* (Thames & Hudson, 1964)

Macmillan, H., *Riding The Storm 1956–1959* (Macmillan, 1971)
McNeill, W. H., *America, Britain and Russia 1941–1946* (Oxford UP, 1953)
Major, J., 'McCarthy and the Communist Witch-Hunt', *History of the 20th Century*, Vol. 6 Ch. 82.
Mao Tse-tung, *Selected Works* Vol. 4 (Foreign Languages Press, Peking 1961)
Marcuse, H., *Soviet Marxism A Critical Analysis* (Penguin, 1971)

Neal, F. W., *US Foreign Policy and the Soviet Union* (Center for the Study of Democratic Institutions, 1961)
Nettl, J. P., *The Soviet Achievement* (Thames & Hudson, 1967)
Northedge, F. S., *British Foreign Policy* (Allen & Unwin, 1962)

O'Ballance, E., *The Greek Civil War* (Faber & Faber, 1966)
Oliva, L. J., *Russia and the West from Peter to Khrushchev* (D. C. Heath & Co., 1965)
Osgood, R. E. *et al*, *America And The World From the Truman Doctrine to Vietnam* (Johns Hopkins, 1970)

Pethybridge, R. W., *A History of Postwar Russia* (Allen & Unwin, 1966)

Reed, J., *Ten Days That Shook The World* (Lawrence & Wishart, 1961)
Rees, D., *The Age of Containment* (Macmillan, 1967)
  Korea: The Limited War (Macmillan, 1964)

Salisbury, H. E., *The Coming War between Russia and China* (Pan Books, 1969)
Sayers, M. and Kahn, A. E., *The Great Conspiracy* (Boni & Gaer, 1947)
Schapiro, L., *The Communist Party of the Soviet Union* (University Paperbacks, 2nd edn. 1970)
Schurmann, F. and Schell, O. (eds.), *Communist China* (Penguin, 1968)
Segal, R., *America's Receding Future* (Penguin, 1970)
Seton-Watson, H., *The Pattern of Communist Revolution* (Methuen, 1953)
Sheehan, N. *et al*, *The Pentagon Papers* (Bantam Books, 1971)
Sherwood, R. E., *The White House Papers of Harry L. Hopkins*, Vol. 1 (Eyre & Spottiswoode, 1948)
  The White House Papers of Harry L. Hopkins, Vol. 2 (Eyre & Spottiswoode, 1949)
Singleton, F. B., *Background to Eastern Europe* (Pergamon Press, 1965)
Smith, H. K., *The State of Europe* (The Cresset Press, 1950)
Snow, E., *Journey to the Beginning* (Gollancz, 1959)
  The Other Side Of The River (Gollancz, 1963)
Spaak, P-H., *Why NATO?* (Penguin, 1959)
Stalin, J. V., *Correspondence with Churchill, Attlee, Roosevelt and Truman* (Lawrence & Wishart, 1958)
Stavrianos, L. S., *The Balkans since 1453* (Rinehart & Co., 1959)
Steel, R., 'Did Anyone Start The Cold War?' (*New York Review of Books*, 2 September 1971)
Stillman, E. and Pfaff, W., *Power and Impotence* (Gollancz, 1966)
  The New Politics (Coward McCann, 1961)
Stone, I. F., *The Hidden History of the Korean War* (Monthly Review Press, 1952. Second Edition 1969)
Stonier, T., *Nuclear Disaster* (Penguin, 1964)

Taylor, A. J. P., *The Origins of the Second World War* (Penguin, 1963)
Thomas, H., *The Spanish Civil War* (Penguin, 1965)
  The Suez Affair (Weidenfeld & Nicolson, 1967)
Toynbee, A., *America and the World Revolution* (Oxford UP, 1962)
Truman, H. S., *Memoirs*, Vol. 1 (Hodder & Stoughton, 1955)
  Memoirs, Vol. 2 (Hodder & Stoughton, 1956)
Tucker, R. W., *Nation Or Empire?* (Johns Hopkins, 1968)

Ulam, A. B., *Expansion and Co-existence* (Secker & Warburg, 1968)
Ullmann, R. H., *Britain and the Russian Civil War* (Oxford UP, 1968)

Watt, D. C. (ed.), *Hitler's Mein Kampf* (Hutchinson, 1969)

Werth, A., *France 1940–1955* (Robert Hale, 1956)
   Russia At War 1941–1945 (Pan Books, 1965)
   Russia: Hopes and Fears (Penguin, 1969)
Wheelwright, E. L. and McFarlane, B., *The Chinese Road to Socialism* (Monthly Review Press, 1970)
   White, T. H., *Fire In The Ashes* (Cassell, 1954)
Whiting, A. S., *China Crosses the Yalu* (Macmillan, 1960)
Williams, F., *A Prime Minister Remembers* (Heinemann, 1961)
Williams, W. A., *The Tragedy of American Diplomacy* (World, 1959)
Wilson, D., *A Quarter of Mankind* (Penguin, 1968)
Windsor, P., 'The Blockade of Berlin', *History of the 20th Century*, Vol. 5 Ch. 77
Wise, D. and Ross, T. B., *The Invisible Government* (Jonathan Cape, 1965)

Zawodny, J. K., *Deaths in the Forest* (University of Notre Dame Press, 1962)

INDEX